New Directions for
Student Services

John H. Schuh
EDITOR-IN-CHIEF

Elizabeth J. Whitt
ASSOCIATE EDITOR

D0743981

Responding to
the Realities of
Race on Campus

Shaun R. Harper
Lori D. Patton
EDITORS

Number 120 • Winter 2007
Jossey-Bass
San Francisco

RESPONDING TO THE REALITIES OF RACE ON CAMPUS
Shaun R. Harper, Lori D. Patton (eds.)
New Directions for Student Services, no. 120
John H. Schuh, Editor-in-Chief
Elizabeth J. Whitt, Associate Editor

NEW DIRECTIONS FOR STUDENT SERVICES (ISSN 0164-7970, e-ISSN 1536-0695) is part of The Jossey-Bass Higher and Adult Education Series and is published quarterly by Wiley Subscription Services, Inc., A Wiley Company, at Jossey-Bass, 989 Market Street, San Francisco, California 94103-1741. Periodicals Postage Paid at San Francisco, California, and at additional mailing offices. POSTMASTER: Send address changes to New Directions for Student Services, Jossey-Bass, 989 Market Street, San Francisco, CA 94103-1741.

New Directions for Student Services is indexed in CIJE: Current Index to Journals in Education (ERIC), Contents Pages in Education (T&F), Current Abstracts (EBSCO), Education Index/Abstracts (H.W. Wilson), Educational Research Abstracts Online (T&F), ERIC Database (Education Resources Information Center), and Higher Education Abstracts (Claremont Graduate University).

Microfilm copies of issues and articles are available in 16mm and 35mm, as well as microfiche in 105mm, through University Microfilms Inc., 300 North Zeeb Road, Ann Arbor, Michigan 48106-1346.

SUBSCRIPTIONS cost $85 for individuals and $209 for institutions, agencies, and libraries in the United States. See ordering information page at end of book.

EDITORIAL CORRESPONDENCE should be sent to the Editor-in-Chief, John H. Schuh, N 243 Lagomarcino Hall, Iowa State University, Ames, Iowa 50011.

Wiley Bicentennial Logo: Richard J. Pacifico

www.josseybass.com

CONTENTS

EDITORS' NOTES

Perhaps a more suitable title for this volume could have been *The Race Card Revisited*. Accusations of exaggeration or unfounded claims often are associated with "pulling the race card." Most often it is persons of color, such as we, who are indicted for attributing what others might perceive to be raceless actions and circumstances to racism and oppression. Inherent in the question, "Why must you always pull the race card?" are erroneous assumptions that race is insignificant; that racism is perceived, not actual; and that racial justice has been achieved. In American higher education, as with the larger society in which colleges and universities exist, many would rather dispose of the race card and avoid uncomfortable conversations about racism.

It has become fashionable for race to be treated as an eruptive topic that gets talked about only when some major crisis occurs on campus, such as a racially motivated hate crime. This mishandling of race in higher education reflects how the general American public deals with the topic. For instance, racism usually attracts the attention of the news media only when celebrities such as former *Seinfeld* actor Michael Richards or radio personality Don Imus make public insulting racist remarks, or when someone such as rapper Kanye West declares on television that the president of the United States does not care about Black people. The reality is that many people, including college students, administrators, and faculty, make racist statements; engage in racially oppressive actions; and maintain exclusive memberships in racially segregated social networks. Such realities are discussed throughout this volume of *New Directions for Student Services*.

This topic seems especially relevant for student affairs and student services because professionals in these areas typically espouse commitments to student learning and development, fostering inclusive campus environments, and retaining diverse populations of college students. Yet failure on the part of student affairs professionals and others to foster critical consciousness about race deprives students of opportunities to learn about what is wrong, offensive, unjust, and oppressive. In a recent public forum pertaining to race at a small liberal arts college, a White male senior repeated the phrase "colored people" as he shared comments with audience members. After being corrected, the student admitted that in his four years on campus, no one had told him this term is outdated and considered offensive by most people of color.

Other examples of such lack of experience or understanding are common. Some student journalists publish racist cartoons in campus newspapers,

NEW DIRECTIONS FOR STUDENT SERVICES, no. 120, Winter 2007 © Wiley Periodicals, Inc.
Published online in Wiley InterScience (www.interscience.wiley.com) • DOI: 10.1002/ss.253

some predominantly White fraternities dress in blackface and host racially offensive theme parties, and conservative student groups sponsor events such as affirmative action bake sales and "Catch an Immigrant Day." In many cases, the students do not recognize that such acts could be deemed racist. More problematic is the fact that most are never challenged to do so.

We assert that it is entirely possible for students to graduate from college without critically reflecting on their racist views, never having engaged in meaningful conversations about race, and using racially offensive language unknowingly. In this way, student affairs educators share responsibility for the reproduction of racially oblivious corporate executives, government and political leaders, and other college graduates who continue to enact laws and manage structures and institutions that maintain White supremacy in the United States. Equally important, when students of color feel marginalized and victimized in racially oppressive environments, they might depart prematurely (Swail, Redd, and Perna, 2003).

Therefore, it would behoove educators and administrators to be more deliberate about assessing and responding to toxic campus racial climates. But for a host of reasons, many would rather not confront the difficult realities of race.

The need to deal with race is not new, nor is the desire to avoid it, but conversations about racism appear to be more taboo than ever before. In order to understand the challenges of approaching dialogues about race, an illustration is warranted. The term "Katrina fatigue," introduced recently, refers to the perception that people (most of them White) are tired of hearing about the devastation of Hurricane Katrina and have grown progressively disinterested in discourse regarding its racial implications.

One might ask, "What does Katrina fatigue have to do with higher education?" Just as persons of privilege can express emotional exhaustion regarding the ongoing destruction resulting from Hurricane Katrina, some student affairs educators and faculty may be fatigued by constant reminders of how students of color find predominantly White colleges and universities racist, alienating, and culturally unresponsive. From their positions of privilege, they lack understanding that the students themselves are probably equally tired of the persistent institutional racism that renders their college experiences oppressive.

What makes people so tired of discussing race, and why do fatigue and frustration ensue? We offer three possible explanations. First, to commit to a discussion about race implies a willingness to deal with guilt, discomfort, and frustration, particularly among those who are privileged by their racial position on college and university campuses. Few White persons, even those who do the good work of student affairs, wish to be reminded that their Whiteness accrues unearned benefits and privileges. Second, discussing race eventually requires coming to terms with the fact that racism is not likely to disappear. Several critical race theorists agree that the most crucial component to understanding race is acceptance that its main byproduct, racism, is a permanent societal fixture so deeply entrenched in structures, systems, and policies that it is difficult to recognize and change (Delgado and Stefancic, 2001; Ladson-Billings and Tate, 1995). "Racial realism" is often perceived as pessimistic. As a consequence, some might ask, "If race is here to stay, then why discuss it?" Derrick Bell (1992), an acclaimed critical race theorist, suggests that acceptance of the permanence of race and racism enables people to work within a more realistic paradigm toward social justice. Despite this, Bergerson (2003) added, "Whites do not want to consider race and racism as everyday realities because doing so requires them to face their own racist behaviors as well as the privileges that come from being White" (p. 53). The editors and contributors to this *New Directions* volume concur with this assertion.

The third reason that conversations about race induce fatigue is that consciousness should lead to personal responsibility. Learning about the detrimental effects of racism and the dichotomy of privilege and oppression should lead to a compulsion to act. Perhaps action is most difficult to deal with because it means surrendering portions of one's own privilege and unearned social assets so that they might be shared with others.

Thus, instead of tackling the realities of race, it is much easier to ignore them by embracing color-blind ideologies. Colorblindness allows people to dismiss the systemic role of oppression instead of blaming overtly racist individuals. It creates a lens through which the existence of race can be denied and the privileges of Whiteness can be maintained without any personal accountability. In addition, colorblind ideologies advance covert, subtle forms of racism that preserve racial inequalities in higher education and society (Forman, 2004).

One byproduct of colorblindness is the continual deracialization of programmatic efforts in higher education and student affairs. Although the student affairs profession remains overwhelmingly White and most graduate preparation programs struggle to attract students of color, the National Association of Student Personnel Administrators' (NASPA) Minority Undergraduate Fellows Program (MUFP) recently removed *minority* from its title and expanded participation beyond racially and ethnically underrepresented populations. While increasing the representation of gay and lesbian people, for example, is both necessary and admirable, goals for improving racial diversity in the profession remain far from realized. It is unlikely that moving beyond MUFP's original aims will yield more professionals of color.

Additional examples of the declining significance of race are the renaming of the magazine formerly known as *Black Issues in Higher Education* to *Diverse Issues in Higher Education*; the inclusion of other populations, such as low-income White students, in retention programs that were once for students of color; and the popular trend of consolidating culture centers for specific racial/ethnic groups into multicultural centers. Although racism, the original –ism in American higher education, remains problematic and unresolved, it has declined in popularity as other –isms (sexism, ableism, ageism, heterosexism, classism, and more) have taken its place and conversations about cultural competence replace discussions about oppression and privilege. Although social justice on behalf of all groups is important, so too are the continual illumination of racial disadvantage and programs and services that focus on race and students of color.

This *New Directions for Student Services* volume presents an opportunity to revisit the race card and reintroduce some racial realities into the consciousness of student affairs practice. In Chapter One, Shaun R. Harper and Sylvia Hurtado synthesize fifteen years of published research on campus racial climates and present nine themes that emerged in their own qualitative study of racial realities at five predominantly White universities. Mitchell J. Chang considers the diversity rationale and cross-racial engagement trends among diverse populations of undergraduates in Chapter Two and recommends moving beyond the artificiality of racial integration on college campuses. A critique of theories commonly taught in graduate preparation programs and an explanation of how critical race theory can be applied to student affairs practice are offered by Lori D. Patton, Marylu McEwen, Laura Rendón, and Mary F. Howard-Hamilton in Chapter Three.

Stephen John Quaye and Marcia B. Baxter Magolda's presentation of ideas for deepening racial self-understanding through structured learning and reflective experiences in Chapter Four is followed by Robert D. Reason and Nancy J. Evans's chapter on constructing racially cognizant campus environments that enable White students to move beyond colorblindness. In Chapter Six, Frank Harris III and Estela Mara Bensimon present the Equity Scorecard as a model for assessing and responding to inequitable outcomes among racially diverse groups of college students. In the final chapter, B. Afeni Cobham and Tara L. Parker discuss the historical evolution of race in higher education, expound on the declining significance of race, and offer some recommendations for resituating race into paradigmatic movements toward multiculturalism and social justice.

We express our sincerest gratitude to the thirteen colleagues who so enthusiastically agreed to contribute to this volume. Despite the politics associated with writing on topics as controversial as race and racism, no author had to be persuaded to extend her or his passion, courage, perspective, and research. Indeed, the chapters that follow can move student affairs and student services into new directions they have long avoided. We appreciate the authors' assistance in helping us revisit the race card in higher education and student affairs boldly. Put simply, Hurricane Katrina presents a pivotal opportunity for faculty and student affairs educators to engage students in dialogues about race, class, and social justice.

Shaun R. Harper
Lori D. Patton
Editors

NEW DIRECTIONS FOR STUDENT SERVICES • DOI: 10.1002/ss

References

Bell, D. A. *Faces at the Bottom of the Well: The Permanence of Racism.* New York: Basic Books, 1992.

Bergerson, A. A. "Critical Race Theory and White Racism: Is There Room for White Scholars in Fighting Racism in Education?" *International Journal of Qualitative Studies in Education,* 2003, *16*(1), 51–63.

Delgado, R., and Stefancic, J. *Critical Race Theory: An Introduction.* New York: New York University Press, 2001.

Forman, T. A. "Colorblind Racism and Racial Indifference: The Role of Racial Apathy in Facilitating Enduring Inequalities." In M. Krysan and A. E. Lewis (eds.), *The Changing Terrain of Race and Ethnicity.* New York: Russell Sage Foundation, 2004.

Ladson-Billings, G., and Tate, W. F. "Toward a Critical Race Theory of Education." *Teachers College Record,* 1995, *97*(1), 47–69.

Swail, W. S., Redd, K. E., and Perna, L. W. *Retaining Minority Students in Higher Education: A Framework for Success. ASHE-ERIC Higher Education Report* (Vol. 30, No. 2). San Francisco: Jossey-Bass, 2003.

SHAUN R. HARPER *is assistant professor of higher education management in the Graduate School of Education at the University of Pennsylvania.*

LORI D. PATTON *is assistant professor of higher education in the Department of Educational Leadership and Policy Studies at Iowa State University.*

1

This chapter synthesizes fifteen years of published research on campus racial climates. It also presents nine themes that emerged from a qualitative study of campus racial climates at five predominantly White universities.

Nine Themes in Campus Racial Climates and Implications for Institutional Transformation

Shaun R. Harper, Sylvia Hurtado

Administrators at two universities were probably less than excited about the news coverage their campuses received on April 27, 2006. Although they were located in different regions of the country, various indicators of racism and racial/ethnic minority student discontent were apparent at both institutions. On one campus in the Northeast, four alarming headlines and race-related stories were printed on the front page of the student newspaper. An incident in which a campus police officer made racist remarks to three African American female students was juxtaposed with the story of a philosophy professor suing the university for demoting him from department chair because he reported to the dean of his college that students had been racially harassed and discriminated against by his faculty colleagues. The third front-page article described a letter sent to the administration by Hillel, the Jewish student organization, demanding an apology and other concessions for the unfair cancellation of a student art exhibit on campus. Among their requests, Hillel student board members asked the university to conduct "an investigation into the discrimination, racism, and intimidation" one of their members experienced in his interactions with the art gallery director.

A protest at the Office of the President organized by Black Caucus and the LGBT (lesbian, gay, bisexual, and transgender) student organization the day before was described in the final story. Protestors said they were insulted

NEW DIRECTIONS FOR STUDENT SERVICES, no. 120, Winter 2007 © Wiley Periodicals, Inc.
Published online in Wiley InterScience (www.interscience.wiley.com) • DOI: 10.1002/ss.254

that staff members locked the office door and the president walked by refusing to address their concerns. Therefore, they slid a letter under the door, chanted outside on megaphones, and subsequently posted a video of the entire protest on YouTube.com. The protest was in response to what students perceived to be insufficient punishment against the women's head basketball coach, a White woman, who allegedly interrogated a Black female player about her sexual orientation, repeatedly threatened to dismiss the student from the team if it was discovered that she was in fact a lesbian, and eventually demanded that the player leave the team. While this story appears to be more about sexual orientation than race, Black Caucus members were especially disturbed that this happened to an African American woman who was probably not the first or only player the coach suspected was gay. Perhaps institutional leaders believed these were isolated incidents that coincidentally occurred around the same time, hence there being no formal assessment of the campus racial climate following this day of problematic news coverage.

With support from the president and provost, the second university commissioned an audit of its campus racial climate. The day after a public presentation of preliminary findings from the audit, a reporter from the city newspaper wrote an article with a bold headline indicating the institution had received "a poor racial report card." The story included a summary of the auditor's findings and this quote from an African American male sophomore: "It is not a sensitive community for Black students. If I stay, the only reason will be to help effect change." The article was also retrieved by the Associated Press and reprinted in newspapers across the nation. Unlike at the first university, administrators on this campus felt public pressure to respond to the problems that had been exposed and were expected to use findings from the racial climate audit to guide institutional change. Within one year, the midwestern school hired a chief diversity officer, crafted a memorandum of understanding with the local chapter of the National Association for the Advancement of Colored People to improve the campus racial climate, organized a conference to examine the status of racial/ethnic minority male students, and pursued more purposefully the recruitment of a diverse faculty, among other efforts. The audit clearly raised institutional consciousness about the realities of race on campus and revealed racial toxins that had long existed but remained unaddressed.

These two predominantly White institutions (PWIs) had similar responses to racial issues on campus. Although the second university was forced to change after having been embarrassed in the local and national press, it is highly unlikely that the audit was the first indicator of racial turbulence on campus. Instead, there had been signals such as those at the first institution that had been disregarded, either intentionally or inadvertently. Unfortunately, such incidents and subsequent responses are not atypical.

In this chapter, we synthesize fifteen years of research about campus racial climates and present nine themes that emerged from a multi-institutional qualitative study we conducted. The primary goal here is to

NEW DIRECTIONS FOR STUDENT SERVICES • DOI: 10.1002/ss

illuminate trends that persist on many college and university campuses, especially those that are predominantly White. At the end of the chapter, we use perspectives on transparency and organizational change to frame our implications for institutional transformation.

Post-1992 Research on Campus Racial Climates

"The Campus Racial Climate: Contexts of Conflict" (Hurtado, 1992) is the most widely cited study on this topic. Results were derived from the Cooperative Institutional Research Program (CIRP) fourth-year follow-up survey, a nationally representative longitudinal study of college students in the late 1980s. Among the most salient findings was that approximately one in four survey respondents perceived considerable racial conflict on their campuses; this proportion was even higher at four-year institutions that were large, public, or selective. When racial conflict was present on campus, few students were convinced that fostering racially diverse learning environments was a high institutional priority. Racial/ethnic minority students were more likely to believe espoused institutional commitments to multiculturalism when racial tension was low. Hurtado also found that White students were less likely than Blacks and Latinos to perceive racial tension on their campuses, as most believed racism was no longer problematic in society. Furthermore, she concluded that racial tension is probable in environments where there is little concern for individual students, which is symptomatic of many large PWIs that enroll several thousand undergraduates.

The Hurtado study has been reprinted in books and frequently cited by scholars who have written about racial realities on college campuses over the past fifteen years. Given the problematic nature of the results presented in this landmark study, we retrieved and analyzed empirical research studies that have since been published in education and social sciences journals to determine how campus racial climates have evolved since 1992. Although considerable effort has been devoted to studying various topics concerning racial/ethnic minority undergraduates at PWIs, we reviewed only journal articles that focused on the racialized experiences of college students and campus racial climates. Also excluded are climate studies regarding racial/ethnic minority faculty and other underrepresented populations (such as LGBT and low-income students), conceptual pieces, literature reviews, unpublished conference papers, dissertations and theses, legal proceedings, reports, and books (with one exception: Feagin, Vera, and Imani, 1996).

Findings from studies that have been published since 1992 can be divided into three categories: (1) differential perceptions of campus climate by race, (2) racial/ethnic minority student reports of prejudicial treatment and racist campus environments, and (3) benefits associated with campus climates that facilitate cross-racial engagement. Studies in which these findings have emerged as well as the methods and samples on which they are based are presented in Table 1.1. Seventy-one percent of the articles we

NEW DIRECTIONS FOR STUDENT SERVICES • DOI: 10.1002/ss

Table 1.1. Clusters of Post-1992 Research Studies on Student Experiences with Race and Campus Racial Climates

Authors	Research Design	Sites	Sample (N)	Respondents/Participants
Differential perceptions of campus climate by race				
Ancis, Sedlacek, and Mohr (2000)	Quantitative	Single	578	Asian American, Black, Latino, and White students
Cabrera and Nora (1994)	Quantitative	Single	879	Asian American, Black, Latino, and White students
Cabrera and others (1999)	Quantitative	Multiple	1,454	Black and White students
D'Augelli and Hershberger (1993)	Quantitative	Single	146	Black and White students
Eimers and Pike (1997)	Quantitative	Single	799	Asian American, Black, Latino, Native American, and White students
Helm, Sedlacek, and Prieto (1998)	Quantitative	Single	566	Asian American, Black, Latino, and White students
Johnson-Durgans (1994)	Quantitative	Single	2,957	Black and White students
Nora and Cabrera (1996)	Quantitative	Single	831	Asian American, Black, Latino, Native American, and White students
Radloff and Evans (2003)	Qualitative	Single	27	Black and White students
Rankin and Reason (2005)	Quantitative	Multiple	7,347	Asian American, Black, Latino, Native American, and White students
Suarez-Balcazar and others (2003)	Quantitative	Single	322	Asian American, Black, Latino, and White students
Racial/ethnic minority student reports of prejudicial treatment and racist campus environments				
Davis and others (2004)	Qualitative	Single	11	Black students
Diver-Stamnes and LoMascolo (2001)	Qualitative	Single	153	Asian American, Black, Latino, Native American, and White students
Feagin, Vera, and Imani (1996)	Qualitative	Single	77	Black students and Parents

NEW DIRECTIONS FOR STUDENT SERVICES • DOI: 10.1002/ss

Study	Method	Single/Multiple	N	Population
Fries-Britt and Turner (2001)	Qualitative	Single	15	Black students
Hurtado (1994a)	Quantitative	Multiple	510	Black and Latino students
Hurtado (1994b)	Quantitative	Multiple	859	Latino students
Hurtado and Carter (1997)	Quantitative	Multiple	272	Latino students
Hurtado, Carter, and Spuler (1996)	Quantitative	Multiple	203	Latino students
Lewis, Chesler, and Forman (2000)	Qualitative	Single	75	Asian American, Black, Latino, and Native American students
Smedley, Myers, and Harrell (1993)	Quantitative	Single	161	Asian American, Black, and Latino students
Solórzano, Ceja, and Yosso (2000)	Qualitative	Multiple	34	Black students
Swim and others (2003)	Mixed	Single	51	Black students
Turner (1994)	Qualitative	Single	32	Asian American, Black, Latino, and Native American students and faculty
Benefits associated with campus climates that facilitate cross-racial engagement				
Antonio (2004)	Qualitative	Single	18	Asian American, Black, Latino, and White students
Antonio and others (2004)	Mixed	Multiple	357	White students
Chang (1999)	Quantitative	Multiple	11,680	Asian American, Black, Latino, and White students
Chang (2001)	Quantitative	Single	167	Asian American, Black, Latino, and White students
Chang, Astin, and Kim (2004)	Quantitative	Multiple	9,703	Asian American, Black, Latino, and White students
Chang, Denson, Sáenz, and Misa (2006)	Quantitative	Multiple	19,667	Asian American, Black, Latino, Native American, and White students
Gurin, Dey, Hurtado, and Gurin (2002)	Quantitative	Multiple	12,965	Asian American, Black, Latino, and White students
Levin, van Laar, and Sidanius (2003)	Quantitative	Single	1,215	Asian American, Black, Latino, and White students
Milem, Umbach, and Liang (2004)	Quantitative	Single	536	White students
Pike and Kuh (2006)	Quantitative	Multiple	42,588	Asian American, Black, Latino, and White students
Sáenz, Ngai, and Hurtado (2007)	Quantitative	Multiple	4,380	Asian American, Black, Latino, and White students

reviewed are based on quantitative methods, and only one qualitative study (Solórzano, Ceja, and Yosso, 2000) was conducted at multiple institutions. Also apparent is that too few researchers have explored how Asian American and Native American students experience campus racial climates. What follows is a brief synopsis of recurring findings within each thematic cluster of studies.

Differential Perceptions of Campus Climate by Race. Researchers have consistently found that racial/ethnic minority students and their White peers who attend the same institution often view the campus racial climate in different ways. For example, racial/ethnic minorities in Rankin and Reason's study (2005) perceived campus climates as more racist and less accepting than did White survey respondents. Similarly, D'Augelli and Hershberger (1993) noted, "Almost all of the sampled African American students reported having borne the brunt of racist remarks and most assumed that African Americans would be mistreated on campus" (p. 77). White students in their study did not report similar experiences and expectations. Nora and Cabrera (1996) found that Whites and racial/ethnic minorities alike perceived the campus climate negatively, reported discrimination from faculty, and recognized insensitivity in the classroom. However, White students' perceptions were weaker on all three measures and not necessarily attributable to race. While both White and Black participants in Cabrera and Nora's study (1994) felt alienated in various ways on campus, racial prejudice and discrimination was the predominant source of such feelings among the latter group.

Radloff and Evans (2003) linked perceptual differences to their participants' home communities. That is, the White students they interviewed grew up in predominantly White neighborhoods and thus had limited firsthand exposure to racism prior to college. Cabrera and others (1999) found that perceptions of racial prejudice had greater effects on Black students' levels of institutional commitment in comparison to their White counterparts who had also experienced various forms of discrimination. Multiple studies have shown that Black students report lower levels of satisfaction with racial climates and perceive differential treatment on the basis of race more frequently than do their Asian American, Latino, Native American, and White peers (Ancis, Sedlacek, and Mohr, 2000; Cabrera and Nora, 1994; Hurtado, 1992; Suarez-Balcazar and others, 2003). These differences are not just in perceptions but also in the way racial/ethnic minority students experience PWIs.

Minority Student Reports of Prejudicial Treatment and Racist Campus Environments. The second cluster of studies, half of them qualitative, offer insights into how racial/ethnic minority students experience race and racism on predominantly White campuses. Consistent with the pre-1992 literature (Allen, 1988; Fleming, 1984; Loo and Rolison, 1986; Nettles, Thoeny, and Gosman, 1986), the research reviewed here consistently calls attention to the isolation, alienation, and stereotyping with which these students are often forced to contend on campuses where they are not the majority. Perhaps the title of Caroline Sotello Viernes Turner's article, "Guests in Someone Else's House: Students of Color" (1994), best characterizes a feeling that is shared among many at most PWIs. In their study of racial/ethnic minority first-year students, Smedley, Myers, and Harrell (1993) discovered that racial conflict and race-laden accusations of intellectual inferiority from White peers and faculty engendered stresses beyond those generally associated with attending a highly selective university; they also found these stresses were most pronounced among Black students. While similar research has focused mostly on undergraduates, Hurtado (1994a) confirmed that Black and Latino graduate students are not immune to the deleterious effects of campus racial climates.

In their study of Latino student transition to college, Hurtado, Carter, and Spuler (1996) suggested, "Even the most talented Latinos are likely to have difficulty adjusting if they perceive a climate where majority students think all minorities are special admits [and] Hispanics feel like they do not 'fit in.' . . . Students may internalize these climate observations, presumably because these are more difficult to identify or sanction than overt forms of discrimination" (p. 152). Reportedly, experiences with racial discrimination and perceptions of racial/ethnic tension complicated the participants' first- and second-year transitions. Beyond the first year, Hurtado and Carter (1997) found that perceptions of racial hostility had negative effects on Latino students' sense of belonging in the junior year of college. In another study (Hurtado, 1994b), 68 percent of the high-achieving Latino students surveyed felt their peers knew very little about Hispanic culture, which significantly increased the participants' feelings of racial/ethnic tension and reports of discriminatory experiences on campus.

Feagin, Vera, and Imani's study (1996) appears to be the first to involve both Black students and parents in an examination of the campus racial climate. Situated at a public university in the Southeast, the participants were well aware of the institution's racist history and the reputation it had garnered for being racially toxic. And the students described the confrontations they had with White peers and faculty, the absence of cultural space they could call their own, barriers to successfully navigating the institution, and the constant burden of disproving racist stereotypes regarding their academic abilities. Fries-Britt and Turner (2001) described how Black students' confidence in their academic abilities is often eroded by stereotypes regarding their intellectual inferiority and presumed entry to universities because of affirmative action.

Black undergraduates participating in a research study by Swim and others (2003) wrote in diaries each time (if at all) they experienced racism or perceived something on their campuses to be racist over a two-week period. Thirty-six percent documented unfriendly looks and skeptical stares from White students and faculty, 24 percent chronicled derogatory and stereotypical verbal remarks directed toward them, 18 percent kept a log of bad service received in the dining hall and other facilities on campus, and 15 percent noted other assorted incidents. The students attributed all of this negative treatment to racism. Solórzano, Ceja, and Yosso (2000) found that when Black students experience racial micro-aggressions (subtle verbal, nonverbal, or visual insults), they begin to feel academically and socially alienated in spaces where such oppression occurs, and as a defense mechanism they create their own academic and social counterspaces (ethnic enclaves that offer shelter from the psycho-emotional harms of racial microaggressions). While the worth of ethnic culture centers, minority student organizations, and other counterspaces has been empirically proven in recent studies (Guiffrida, 2003; Harper and Quaye, 2007; Patton, 2006; Solórzano and Villalpando, 1998), a reality is that they often limit interactions between White students and racial/ethnic minorities.

Benefits Associated with Campus Climates That Facilitate Cross-Racial Engagement. Findings from studies in the third cluster are relatively consistent. Researchers have recently furnished a large body of empirical evidence to confirm the educational merit of deliberately creating racially diverse college campuses. Much of this evidence was used in support of testimony for the University of Michigan affirmative action cases (*Gratz* v. *Bollinger* and *Grutter* v. *Bollinger*). These studies verify that students who attend racially diverse institutions and are engaged in educationally purposeful activities that involve interactions with peers from different racial/ethnic backgrounds come to enjoy cognitive, psychosocial, and interpersonal gains that are useful during and after college (Antonio and others, 2004; Chang, 1999, 2001; Chang, Astin, and Kim, 2004; Chang, Denson, Sáenz, and Misa, 2006; Gurin, Dey, Hurtado, and Gurin, 2002; Pike and Kuh, 2006).

Exposure to diverse perspectives during college could interrupt long-standing segregation trends in society. Students (especially Whites) who engage meaningfully with peers from different backgrounds and diverse perspectives both inside and outside college classrooms are unlikely to remain isolated within their own racial/ethnic communities (Sáenz, Nagi, and Hurtado, 2007), which is believed to be sustainable in environments (such as residential neighborhoods) after college (Milem, Umbach, and Liang, 2004). In contrast to those who maintained racially homogeneous friendships, undergraduates (especially first-year students) with friends outside their race held fewer biases about and expressed less anxiety toward racially different others at the end of college (Levin, van Laar, and Sidanius, 2003). Participants in Antonio's study on friendship grouping (2004) agreed their campus was racially segregated and could describe the range of racially homogeneous groups that existed. Despite this, many selected best friends based on those with whom they interacted most in the first year of college, not on the basis of race. These findings illustrate the importance of institutional intent in creating spaces and opportunities for meaningful cross-racial engagement, especially for students who are newcomers to an institution.

A Multicampus Qualitative Study of Racial Climates

Solórzano, Ceja, and Yosso's article (2000) appears to be the only published qualitative study of racial climates based on data collected from more than one institution. It should be noted that their sample was composed exclusively of Black students. To explore the realities of race more deeply, we used qualitative research methods at five PWIs located in three different geographical regions of the country; two campuses were in rural towns and the others in urban areas. In light of Hurtado's finding (1992) that institutional size affects perceptions of the campus racial climate, only large institutions were included in this study. On average, White students composed 73 percent of the undergraduate populations on these campuses. The primary goals were to pursue a deeper understanding of how contemporary cohorts of students experience campus racial climates in the three areas consistently noted in the literature, while searching for additional themes that have not been captured as fully in previous research.

Focus groups were facilitated with 278 Asian American, Black, Latino, Native American, and White students across the five campuses. The composition of each focus group was racially homogeneous (for example, only Native Americans in one and Latinos exclusively in another). Administrators in academic affairs, student affairs, and multicultural affairs assisted in participant recruitment by sending mass e-mail invitations to all undergraduates from each of the racial/ethnic minority populations on the campus; each White participant led a major campus organization such as student government. In addition to interviews with students, one additional focus group was facilitated with staff persons (mostly entry- and midlevel professionals) from academic affairs, student affairs, and multicultural affairs at each institution. Interestingly, only five of the forty-one staff participants were White, even though we never specified a preference for racial/ethnic minorities who worked at the institutions.

Each focus group session was audiorecorded and later transcribed. The interview transcripts were analyzed using the NVivo Qualitative Data Analysis Software Program. Several techniques prescribed by Miles and Huberman (1994) and Moustakas (1994) were systematically employed to analyze the data collected in this study. The analyses led to the identification of nine recurring themes, which are presented in the next section. To ensure the trustworthiness of the data, we shared our findings in public forums on each campus where participants were invited to deny or confirm our syntheses of what they reported in focus groups about the racial climate, a technique referred to as "member checks" (Lincoln and Guba, 1986). Patton (2002) noted that participants with seemingly unpopular or minority points of view might not feel empowered to offer divergent perspectives in focus groups and subsequently may decide against reporting something different or controversial, a trend better known as "focus group effect." This certainly could have been the case in this study and is therefore acknowledged as a limitation.

New Directions for Student Services • DOI: 10.1002/ss

Using a different sampling and participant recruitment technique for White students, while justified below, is another noteworthy shortcoming.

Each of the five campuses in this study had its own context-specific challenges with race and racism, which are not discussed here to keep the institutions' identities anonymous. Instead, we present and summarize nine common racial realities across the institutions.

Cross-Race Consensus Regarding Institutional Negligence. Racial/ethnic minorities and White students alike expressed frustration with the incongruence of espoused and enacted institutional values concerning diversity. "The university has diversity plastered everywhere, but I have yet to see any real evidence of it," one focus group participant commented. Many were also disappointed with the lofty expectation that they would magically interact across racial difference on their own. A White student told of growing up on a ranch in Texas where he had not interacted with anyone outside his race prior to enrolling at the university. Regarding the initiation of conversations with racial/ethnic minorities on the campus, he asked: "Why should I be expected to know how to do this on my own? And the university expects us to talk about something as sensitive as racism without helping us. This is unrealistic and actually unfair." Other students wanted and needed assistance, structure, and venues in which to meaningfully engage with racially different peers, but they found little guidance from educators and administrators. Consequently, almost all of the students interviewed deemed their institutions negligent in the educational processes leading to racial understanding, both inside and outside the classroom.

Race as a Four-Letter Word and an Avoidable Topic. Participants, including the staff persons interviewed, spoke of the infrequency with which race-related conversations occurred on their campuses. Put simply, race remained an unpopular topic and was generally considered taboo in most spaces, including classes other than ethnic studies. At one institution, a midlevel staff member shared: "We don't talk about race on this campus because this state has long struggled with racial issues that trace back to slavery. So the political climate is such that the university would get into trouble with the state legislators if we talked too much about race." Students also referenced city and state political norms in their comments about the silencing of topics related to racism and racial injustice. "This campus is a microcosm of [this town] when it comes to running away from anything that even smells like race. It is just something we never talk about here, and most people are okay with that." Many participants recognized the contradiction inherent in expecting students to interact across racial lines on campuses where race is deliberately unacknowledged in classrooms and other structured venues.

Self-Reports of Racial Segregation. Like the students in Antonio's study (2004), participants here were well aware of the segregation on their campuses. Few encountered difficulty naming spaces where evidence of racial segregation could be found. Chief among them was fraternity row. In fact, one Black student referred to this segregated space as "Jim Crow Row," as he reflected on fraternity parties and other events to which he had been denied access, perceivably due to his race. At the conclusion of a focus group at another institution, the participants led a guided tour through various "ethnic neighborhoods" (as they called them) in the campus dining hall, where racial segregation was visibly apparent. Beyond observable segregation trends on the campuses, most students we interviewed personally confessed to having few (if any) friends from different racial/ethnic backgrounds. Several White participants expressed an interest in building friendships with others but said they did not know how. By her own admission, a White female student leader was embarrassed that she had not even noticed until the focus group discussion that all of her close friends were White. In some instances, White students attributed their lack of engagement with racial/ethnic minority peers to the existence of minority student organizations. "If we did not have the Black frats, our chapters would have more diverse members," an Interfraternity Council president claimed. Worth acknowledging here is that only twenty-nine students held membership in the four Black fraternities on this particular campus.

Gaps in Social Satisfaction by Race. White and Asian American students often expressed feelings of social satisfaction at the five institutions and found it difficult to identify aspects of the campus environment they would change. Because all the White participants were student leaders, the universality of this finding should be interpreted with caution. While not as satisfied as the White and Asian American students, Latinos and Native Americans mostly expressed gratitude for having been afforded the opportunity to matriculate at the various campuses. Their expectations for the provision of stronger social support appeared to be modest in comparison to those of their Black peers. It should be noted that Native American undergraduates were less than half of 1 percent of the undergraduate student populations on four of the campuses we studied. In one focus group, a Latina first-year student began with an enthusiastic description of the benefits associated with attending such a prestigious university, but hearing stories from others ignited consciousness of just how little social support she had been afforded at the institution. At every university, Black students expressed the highest degrees of dissatisfaction with the social environment.

Reputational Legacies for Racism. One logical explanation for Black student displeasure was the bad reputations that preceded the universities they attended. Some entered their institutions expecting to experience racism. "My parents, sister, aunt, and just about every African American in my home town couldn't understand why I came here. They told me to go to [a black college] because this place is so racist," one woman shared. In each focus group, other Black students told similar stories of how they had been warned about the racist environments they would encounter. "Kanye West said George W. Bush does not care about Black people. Well, it is obvious [this institution] does not care about Black people, and we have known this for a few generations now." Like the students and parents in Feagin, Vera, and Imani's study (1996), Black undergraduates interviewed for this study described how negatively their institutions were viewed within Black communities across the state because of historical exclusionary admissions practices. Many Black students withdrew prematurely in the past, and those who managed to persist through degree attainment often returned to their home communities with stories of the racism they had endured. Although this was found only among Black students in the study, its salience and consistency across the five campuses makes it noteworthy.

White Student Overestimation of Minority Student Satisfaction. White student leaders were selected because they were thought to be most likely to have interacted with racial/ethnic minority peers in the student organizations they led. Moreover, we suspected they were positioned to offer more meaningful appraisals of the campus racial climates because of their levels of political leadership on the campuses. Focus groups with these participants were always conducted after those with racial/ethnic minority students. The White students were most satisfied with the social environments, and they erroneously assumed their Black, Latino, and Native American peers experienced the institutions this same way. They reported that racial/ethnic minority student engagement in mainstream campus organizations was low, but for some reason those students were thought to be equally satisfied with their college experiences. When asked about the basis of their assumptions, the White participants often responded with, "I don't know . . . I just figured everyone loves it here." Because there was so little structured and meaningful interaction across races, student leaders who were presumed to have understood the general pulse of the campus were generally unaware of the disparate affective dispositions their racial/ethnic minority peers held toward the institutions.

The Pervasiveness of Whiteness in Space, Curricula, and Activities. Beyond ethnic and multicultural centers on the five campuses, Asian American, Black, Latino, and Native American students found it difficult to identify other spaces on campus in which they felt shared cultural ownership. White interests were thought to be privileged over others, which many racial/ethnic minorities viewed as inconsistent with institutional claims of inclusiveness. These perceptions are perhaps best illustrated in this quote from a sophomore student: "Everything is so White. The concerts: White musicians. The activities: catered to White culture. The football games: a ton of drunk White folks. All the books we read in class: White authors and viewpoints. Students on my left, right, in front and in back of me in my classes: White, White, White, White. I feel like there is nothing for us here besides the [cultural] center, but yet [this university] claims to be so big on diversity. That is the biggest white lie I have ever heard." Other participants also critiqued the isolation of ethnic culture to a single center, office, or academic major. Although Asian American students generally appeared to be as satisfied as their White peers, even they expressed a desire for greater cultural representation.

The Consciousness-Powerlessness Paradox among Racial/Ethnic Minority Staff. Nearly 88 percent of the staff persons we interviewed were racial/ethnic minorities. Interestingly, they were fully aware of the degree to which minority students were disadvantaged and dissatisfied on the five campuses. They also knew about the extent to which racial segregation existed. Much of what the students shared in focus groups was confirmed (mostly without prompting) in interviews with the staff. One of the five White staff participants asserted, "Everyone around this table knows how segregated students are, but we never talk about it. It is the sort of thing that will piss the upper administration off and make them leery of you for raising the issue." Despite their consciousness of the realities of race, most indicated a reluctance to publicly call attention to these trends for fear of losing their jobs or political backlash. "I feel bad for what the young brothers and sisters go through here, but there is only so much I can do since I have only been here two years," a Latino academic advisor explained. Staff persons would complain to each other and privately strategize with students but felt powerless in voicing observations to senior administrators and White colleagues. Fear of being seen as troublemakers who were always calling attention to racism compelled many to remain silent.

Unexplored Qualitative Realities of Race in Institutional Assessment. In every focus group on each of the five campuses, student participants (Whites and racial/ethnic minorities alike) indicated that it was the first time any institutional effort was made to inquire about the qualitative realities of their racialized experiences. "You're the first person to ask us these kinds of questions" was a common remark. Furthermore, the White student leaders said no one, including their student organization advisors, had ever asked them questions about minority student engagement and satisfaction or the frequency with which they interacted with peers who were racially different. Reportedly, the institutional research offices had not conducted any formal climate assessments. Likewise, informal queries from faculty and administrators were also uncommon. "If they truly cared, they would have asked us about these things before now," a Native American male senior believed.

Implications for Institutional Transformation

The 2006 report of the commission appointed by U.S. Department of Education Secretary Margaret Spellings to explore needed areas of improvement in higher education called for more transparency regarding student learning outcomes on college and university campuses. Merely reporting outcomes, however, keeps the source of racial inequities undisclosed and does not result in better, more inclusive climates for learning. The consistency of results from fifteen years of empirical research, along with the nine themes that emerged in our study, make clear the need for greater transparency regarding racial realities in learning environments at PWIs. Even when cues are readily available (for example, a newspaper with four front-page articles related to racial injustice), the realities of race are typically made transparent only when there is a highly publicized, racially motivated incident or when embarrassing findings from an external auditor are made public.

Consistent with Kezar and Eckel's recommendation (2002a), we suggest that administrators, faculty, and institutional researchers proactively audit their campus climates and cultures to determine the need for change. As indicated in many of the nine themes, racial realities remained undisclosed and unaddressed in systematic ways on college campuses. As long as administrators espouse commitments to diversity and multiculturalism without engaging in examinations of campus climates, racial/ethnic minorities will continue to feel dissatisfied, all students will remain deprived of the full range of educational benefits accrued through cross-racial engagement, and certain institutions will sustain longstanding reputations for being racially toxic environments.

Eckel and Kezar (2003) defined *transformation* as the type of change that affects the institutional culture, is deep and pervasive, is intentional, and occurs over time. Accordingly, deep change reflects a shift in values (for example, from espoused to enacted) and assumptions that underlie daily operations (for example, the flawed expectation that cross-racial interactions will magically occur on their own). Pervasiveness indicates that change is felt across the institution in the assumptions and daily work of faculty, staff, and administrators. For example, the Black culture center on a campus cannot improve an institution's external reputation if professors routinely perpetuate racist stereotypes in classrooms. Also, racial/ethnic minority students will continue to feel like "guests in someone else's house" if student activities offices fail to sponsor programs that reflect the diverse cultures represented on a campus. Intentionality in constructing culturally affirming environments and experiences that facilitate the cultivation of racially diverse friendship groups must substitute passivity and negligence. As previous research has established, these racial climate issues have consequences for student outcomes (Hurtado, Milem, Clayton-Pedersen, and Allen, 1998). For example, attention to diversity in the curriculum and cocurriculum, particularly in the first two years of college, results in student development along many dimensions of complex thinking and social cognitive growth (Hurtado, 2005).

Eckel and Kezar (2003) also distinguished transformation from other types of change, including adjustments that continually happen in academia that are neither pervasive nor deep, such as showing a one-hour video on respecting diversity at new student orientation; isolated change that may be deep but limited to one unit or program area, as when an ethnic studies department offers a cluster of elective courses on race; or far-reaching change that affects many across the institution but lacks depth, as with a policy regarding the symbolic inclusion of an equal opportunity statement on letterhead and all hiring materials. Moreover, Kezar and Eckel (2002b) found that senior administrative support, collaboration, and visible action are among the core elements requisite for transformational change in higher education. While administrative leadership on its own is insufficient, our findings make clear that entry- and midlevel professionals, especially racial/ethnic minorities, often feel silenced and powerless to transform campus racial climates.

In their 2005 study, Kezar and Eckel interviewed thirty college presidents who had been engaged in organizational change with a significant emphasis on the success of racial/ethnic minority students. The presidents used a strategy of dialogue and discussion in the appraisal of their own and their institutions' commitments to diversity, while holding various stakeholders accountable for aligning efforts with stated institutional values and priorities. If this is to occur on other campuses, race cannot remain an avoidable topic. For instance, if accountability for student learning is a high priority, dialogue and strategic efforts must be directed toward addressing undercurrents of racial segregation that inhibit the rich learning that occurs in cross-racial engagement. Likewise, faculty and staff in academic affairs, student affairs, multicultural affairs, and other units on campus should be challenged to consider their roles as accomplices in the cyclical reproduction of racism and institutional negligence.

Despite fifteen years of racial climate research on multiple campuses, the themes of exclusion, institutional rhetoric rather than action, and marginality continue to emerge from student voices. Conducting a climate study can be symbolic of institutional action, only to be filed away on a shelf. We advocate that data gathered through the ongoing assessment of campus racial climates guide conversations and reflective examinations to overcome discomfort with race, plan for deep levels of institutional transformation, and achieve excellence in fostering racially inclusive learning environments.

References

Allen, W. R. "Black Students in U.S. Higher Education: Toward Improved Access, Adjustment, and Achievement." *Urban Review,* 1988, *20*(3), 165–188.

Ancis, J. R., Sedlacek, W. E., and Mohr, J. J. "Student Perceptions of Campus Cultural Climate by Race." *Journal of Counseling and Counseling Development,* 2000, *78,* 180–185.

Antonio, A. L. "When Does Race Matter in College Friendships? Exploring Men's Diverse and Homogeneous Friendship Groups." *Review of Higher Education,* 2004, *27*(4), 553–575.

Antonio, A. L., and others. "Effects of Racial Diversity on Complex Thinking in College Students." *Psychological Science,* 2004, *15*(8), 507–510.

Cabrera, A. F., and Nora, A. "College Students' Perceptions of Prejudice and Discrimination and Their Feelings of Alienation: A Construct Validation Approach." *Review of Education/Pedagogy/Cultural Studies,* 1994, *16*(3), 387–409.

Cabrera, A. F., and others. "Campus Racial Climate and the Adjustment of Students to College: A Comparison Between White Students and African American Students." *Journal of Higher Education,* 1999, *70*(2), 134–160.

Chang, M. J. "Does Racial Diversity Matter? The Educational Impact of a Racially Diverse Undergraduate Population." *Journal of College Student Development*, 1999, *40*(4), 377–395.

Chang, M. J. "Is It More Than About Getting Along? The Broader Educational Relevance of Reducing Students' Racial Biases." *Journal of College Student Development*, 2001, *42*(2), 93–105.

Chang, M. J., Astin, A. W., and Kim, D. "Cross-Racial Interaction Among Undergraduates: Some Consequences, Causes and Patterns." *Research in Higher Education*, 2004, *45*(5), 529–553.

Chang, M. J., Denson, N., Sáenz, V., and Misa, K. "The Educational Benefits of Sustaining Cross-Racial Interaction Among Undergraduates." *Journal of Higher Education*, 2006, *77*(3), 430–455.

D'Augelli, A. R., and Hershberger, S. L. "African American Undergraduates on a Predominantly White Campus: Academic Factors, Social Networks, and Campus Climate." *Journal of Negro Education*, 1993, *62*(1), 67–81.

Davis, M., and others. "'A Fly in the Buttermilk': Descriptions of University Life by Successful Black Undergraduate Students at a Predominately White Southeastern University." *Journal of Higher Education*, 2004, *75*(4), 420–445.

Diver-Stamnes, A. C., and LoMascolo, A. F. "The Marginalization of Ethnic Minority Students: A Case Study of a Rural University." *Equity and Excellence in Education*, 2001, *34*(1), 50–58.

Eckel, P. D., and Kezar, A. J. *Taking the Reins: Institutional Transformation in Higher Education.* Westport, Conn.: Praeger, 2003.

Eimers, M. T., and Pike, G. R. "Minority and Nonminority Adjustment to College: Differences or Similarities?" *Research in Higher Education*, 1997, *38*(1), 77–97.

Feagin, J. R., Vera, H., and Imani, N. *The Agony of Education: Black Students at White Colleges and Universities.* New York: Routledge, 1996.

Fleming, J. *Blacks in College: A Comparative Study of Students' Success in Black and White Institutions.* San Francisco: Jossey-Bass, 1984.

Fries-Britt, S. L., and Turner, B. "Facing Stereotypes: A Case Study of Black Students on a White Campus." *Journal of College Student Development*, 2001, *42*(5), 420–429.

Gratz v. *Bollinger*, 123 2411 (S. Ct. 2003).

Grutter v. *Bollinger*, 124 35 (S. Ct. 2003).

Guiffrida, D. A. "African American Student Organizations as Agents of Social Integration." *Journal of College Student Development*, 2003, *44*(3), 304–319.

Gurin, P., Dey, E. L., Hurtado, S., and Gurin, G. "Diversity and Higher Education: Theory and Impact on Educational Outcomes." *Harvard Educational Review*, 2002, *72*(3), 330–366.

Harper, S. R., and Quaye, S. J. "Student Organizations as Venues for Black Identity Expression and Development Among African American Male Student Leaders." *Journal of College Student Development*, 2007, *48*(2), 127–144.

Helm, E. G., Sedlacek, W. E., and Prieto, D. O. "The Relationship Between Attitudes Toward Diversity and Overall Satisfaction of University Students by Race." *Journal of College Counseling*, 1998, *1*, 111–120.

Hurtado, S. "The Campus Racial Climate: Contexts of Conflict." *Journal of Higher Education*, 1992, *63*(5), 539–569.

Hurtado, S. "Graduate School Racial Climates and Academic Self-Concept Among Minority Graduate Students in the 1970s." *American Journal of Education*, 1994a, *102*(3), 330–351.

Hurtado, S. "The Institutional Climate for Talented Latino Students." *Research in Higher Education*, 1994b, *35*(1), 21–41.

Hurtado, S. "The Next Generation of Diversity and Intergroup Relations Research." *Journal of Social Issues*, 2005, *61*(3), 595–610.

Hurtado, S., and Carter, D. F. "Effects of College Transition and Perceptions of the Campus Racial Climate on Latino College Students' Sense of Belonging." *Sociology of Education,* 1997, *70*(4), 324–345.

Hurtado, S., Carter, D. F., and Spuler, A. "Latino Student Transition to College: Assessing Difficulties and Factors in Successful College Adjustment." *Research in Higher Education,* 1996, *37*(2), 135–157.

Hurtado, S., Milem, J. F., Clayton-Pedersen, A., and Allen, W. R. "Enhancing Campus Climates for Racial/Ethnic Diversity: Educational Policy and Practice." *Review of Higher Education,* 1998, *21*(3), 279–302.

Johnson-Durgans, V. D. "Perceptions of Racial Climates in Residence Halls Between African American and Euroamerican College Students." *Journal of College Student Development,* 1994, *35*(4), 267–274.

Kezar, A. J., and Eckel, P. D. "The Effect of Institutional Culture on Change Strategies in Higher Education: Universal Principles or Culturally Responsive Concepts?" *Journal of Higher Education,* 2002a, *73*(4), 435–460.

Kezar, A. J., and Eckel, P. D. "Examining the Institutional Transformation Process: The Importance of Sensemaking, Interrelated Strategies, and Balance." *Research in Higher Education,* 2002b, *43*(3), 295–328.

Kezar, A. J., and Eckel, P. D. *Leadership Strategies for Advancing Campus Diversity: Advice from Experienced Presidents.* Washington, D.C.: American Council on Education, 2005.

Levin, S., van Larr, C., and Sidanius, J. "The Effects of Ingroup and Outgroup Friendships on Ethnic Attitudes in College: A Longitudinal Study." *Group Processes and Intergroup Relations,* 2003, *6*(1), 76–92.

Lewis, A. E., Chesler, M., and Forman, T. A. "The Impact of 'Colorblind' Ideologies on Students of Color: Intergroup Relations at a Predominantly White University." *Journal of Negro Education,* 2000, *69*(1), 74–91.

Lincoln, Y., and Guba, E. G. "But Is It Rigorous? Trustworthiness and Authenticity in Naturalistic Evaluation." In D. William (ed.), *Naturalistic Evaluation.* New Directions for Program Evaluation, no. 30. San Francisco: Jossey-Bass, 1986.

Loo, C. M., and Rolison, G. "Alienation of Ethnic Minority Students at a Predominantly White University." *Journal of Higher Education,* 1986, *57*(1), 58–77.

Milem, J. F., Umbach, P. D., and Liang, C.T.H. "Exploring the Perpetuation Hypothesis: The Role of Colleges and Universities in Desegregating Society." *Journal of College Student Development,* 2004, *45*(6), 688–700.

Miles, M. B., and Huberman, A. M. *Qualitative Data Analysis: An Expanded Sourcebook.* (2nd ed.) Thousand Oaks, Calif.: Sage, 1994.

Moustakas, C. *Phenomenological Research Methods.* Thousand Oaks, Calif.: Sage, 1994.

Nettles, M. T., Thoeny, A. R., and Gosman, E. J. "Comparative and Predictive Analyses of Black and White Students' Achievement and Experiences." *Journal of Higher Education,* 1986, *57*(3), 289–318.

Nora, A., and Cabrera, A. F. "The Role of Perceptions of Prejudice and Discrimination on the Adjustment of Minority Students to College." *Journal of Higher Education,* 1996, *67*(2), 119–148.

Patton, L. D. "The Voice of Reason: A Qualitative Examination of Black Student Perceptions of Black Culture Centers." *Journal of College Student Development,* 2006, *47*(6), 628–644.

Patton, M. Q. *Qualitative Research and Evaluation Methods.* (3rd ed.) Thousand Oaks, Calif.: Sage, 2002.

Pike, G. R., and Kuh, G. D. "Relationships Among Structural Diversity, Informal Peer Interactions, and Perceptions of the Campus Environment." *Review of Higher Education,* 2006, *29*(4), 425–450.

Radloff, T. D., and Evans, N. J. "The Social Construction of Prejudice Among Black and White College Students." *NASPA Journal,* 2003, *40*(2), 1–16.

Rankin, S. R., and Reason, R. D. "Differing Perceptions: How Students of Color and White Students Perceive Campus Climate for Underrepresented Groups." *Journal of College Student Development,* 2005, *46*(1), 43–61.

Sáenz, V. B., Nagi, H. N., and Hurtado, S. "Factors Influencing Positive Interactions Across Race for African American, Asian American, Latino, and White College Students." *Research in Higher Education,* 2007, *48*(1), 1–38.

Smedley, B. D., Myers, H. F., and Harrell, S. P. "Minority-Status Stresses and the College Adjustment of Ethnic Minority Freshmen." *Journal of Higher Education,* 1993, *64*(4), 434–452.

Solórzano, D., Ceja, M., and Yosso, T. J. "Critical Race Theory, Racial Microaggressions, and Campus Racial Climate: The Experiences of African American College Students." *Journal of Negro Education,* 2000, *69*(1), 60–73.

Solórzano, D., and Villalpando, O. "Critical Race Theory: Marginality and the Experience of Students of Color in Higher Education." In C. A. Torres and T. R. Mitchell (eds.), *Sociology of Education: Emerging Perspectives.* Albany: State University of New York Press, 1998.

Suarez-Balcazar, Y., and others. "Experiences of Differential Treatment Among College Students of Color." *Journal of Higher Education,* 2003, *74*(4), 428–444.

Swim, J. K., and others. "African American College Students' Experiences with Everyday Racism: Characteristics of and Responses to These Incidents." *Journal of Black Psychology,* 2003, *29*(1), 38–67.

Turner, C.S.V. "Guests in Someone Else's House: Students of Color." *Review of Higher Education,* 1994, *17*(4), 355–370.

U.S. Department of Education. *A Test of Leadership, Charting the Future of U.S. Higher Education: A Report of the Commission Appointed by Secretary of Education Margaret Spellings.* Washington, D.C.: U.S. Department of Education, 2006.

SHAUN R. HARPER *is assistant professor of higher education management in the Graduate School of Education at the University of Pennsylvania.*

SYLVIA HURTADO *is professor of higher education and organizational change and director of the Higher Education Research Institute at the University of California, Los Angeles.*

NEW DIRECTIONS FOR STUDENT SERVICES • DOI: 10.1002/ss

2

In this chapter, the challenges associated with engaging race and encouraging cross-racial interactions among students are examined. Readers are invited to reimagine the role that higher education and student affairs could play in improving racial dynamics and relations among students.

Beyond Artificial Integration: Reimagining Cross-Racial Interactions Among Undergraduates

Mitchell J. Chang

When the movie *Crash* received the Oscar for Best Picture at the seventy-eighth Academy Awards, an important spotlight was cast on race relations in the United States. Surely the movie did not receive this recognition for artistic qualities alone. The race problems depicted in the film engendered emotion and awakened consciousness among many who saw it, reinforcing the need to respond to racial "crashes" in society. Many educators have long argued that colleges and universities can make a significant difference in improving how race is treated in the United States. It also turns out that addressing this problem can more broadly add statistically measurable value to students' educational experiences and learning in college. However, higher education's capacity to address this significant and enduring national problem has been constrained in ways that at times make those institutions and the individuals who attend them part of the problem rather than the solution.

This chapter highlights the many challenges and obstacles that limit and undermine higher education's capacity to eradicate the negative consequences associated with race. Before discussing these challenges, I address why it makes sense for colleges and universities to play a central role in addressing problems associated with race. Then I discuss some pitfalls that limit the capacity of these institutions to make a difference and ultimately steer us toward what I have termed *artificial integration*. I conclude by suggesting a reimagination of racial integration to help professionals in higher

NEW DIRECTIONS FOR STUDENT SERVICES, no. 120, Winter 2007 © Wiley Periodicals, Inc.
Published online in Wiley InterScience (www.interscience.wiley.com) • DOI: 10.1002/ss.255

education and student affairs envision a new direction toward improving racial dynamics and race relations.

This chapter is not intended to be a comprehensive literature review, but draws mostly from my own research that has primarily focused on diversity-related topics for over a decade. Thus, I neither rigorously support nor refute claims with a more comprehensive account of the larger body of literature, which is beyond the scope of this chapter. Still, I believe some important insights can be drawn from this more focused body of work.

The Diversity Rationale

It is not difficult to ascertain why some educators have grown increasingly more pessimistic about whether higher education can aid in eradicating the negative effects associated with race. After all, modern civil rights legislation has been in place for over four decades, and although some progress has been made, much more still needs to be done. The hope of solving what W.E.B. DuBois (1903) called the "race problem" within the time frame of one generation, let alone two, has not been realized. The challenges continue to be daunting, and the results of many fervent efforts are not always obvious. Given the circumstances that can easily engender pessimism, it may be worth noting why those in higher education should not yield but instead try harder to make a difference. The call for more intense efforts to address race is still compelling. Much seems to be riding on our nation's capacity to improve the combination of economic, political, ideological, cultural, and social forces that give meaning to race, or what I refer to as racial dynamics. Racial dynamics shape the ways in which individuals of different races interact and relate to each other, or what I refer to as race relations.

Support for improving such forces can be seen in the record number of amicus briefs submitted to buttress the University of Michigan's defense of race-conscious admissions practices (*Gratz* v. *Bollinger* and *Grutter* v. *Bollinger*). Because there are so many well-noted social and moral imperatives for why educational institutions must address both racial dynamics and race relations (see, for example, Chang, Witt, Jones, and Hakuta, 2003), I am highlighting here one specific line of arguments that makes an educational case. Often referred to as the diversity rationale, these arguments have played a central role in the legal defense of race-conscious admissions practices in higher education. I focus on this rationale not because it is necessarily more important or compelling than others (in fact, quite the contrary), but because I have studied it extensively and understand some of its strengths and weaknesses (Chang, Chang, and Ledesma, 2005; Chang, 2005; Moses and Chang, 2006).

The diversity rationale has had a unique course of development in the U.S. Supreme Court's deliberations. Although Supreme Court Justice Lewis Powell was not the first to recognize the added value that diversity brings to educational settings, he was first to apply the diversity rationale as a justification for defending race-conscious admissions practices. His reasoning appeared in his 1978 opinion regarding the *Bakke* v. *Regents of the University of California*. Briefly stated, Powell viewed the interest of providing educational benefits associated with a diverse student body as a permissible basis for the consideration of race in university admissions practices. The appropriateness of the rationale to justify the use of race in admitting students continues to be a matter of legal controversy. In 2003, however, a majority of the U.S. Supreme Court in their decision in *Grutter* v. *Bollinger* considered this rationale to be a valid justification for applying certain types of race-conscious admissions policies.

The Court that decided *Grutter* appeared to be more confident than Justice Powell was in *Bakke* regarding the benefits that stem from a diverse student body. For example, in the *Grutter* majority opinion, Justice Sandra Day O'Connor claimed, "These benefits are not theoretical *but real,* as major American businesses have made clear that the skills needed in today's increasingly global marketplace can only be developed through exposure to widely diverse people, cultures, ideas, and viewpoints." The Court was ostensibly moved by those who stepped forward to testify in favor of diversity, which included hundreds of the nation's most prestigious Fortune 500 corporations, high-ranking retired military personnel, scholarly organizations, and educators, among others. The body of research evidence cited by O'Connor did indeed suggest that Powell was on to something. Although Powell had a solid intuitive grasp of how increased racial diversity in a student body contributes in educationally meaningful ways, he failed to account for the process necessary to realize those added benefits for students.

Cross-Racial Engagement and Educational Outcomes

Since the resolution of the Michigan cases, I joined Jeffrey Milem and Anthony Lising Antonio (2005) to synthesize some of the empirical research associated with the diversity rationale in an Association of American Colleges and Universities publication, *Making Diversity Work on Campus: A Research-Based Perspective*. We generally concluded in this synthesis of the research literature that increasing racial diversity in the student body furthers the broad educational mission of institutions of higher education by offering new opportunities for student learning, advancing students' existing knowledge, and preparing them to better serve society as workers, citizens, and leaders. We argued that because racial differences are often associated with diverse viewpoints and opinions, an increase in the proportion of underrepresented students can bring to a university experiences, outlooks, and ideas that can potentially enhance the educational experiences of all students. The overall educational impact of racial diversity, however, seems to be largely determined by the levels of student engagement or involvement. Thus, the impact is likely to be strongest when campuses

New Directions for Student Services • DOI: 10.1002/ss

intervene by coordinating a set of mutually supportive and reinforcing experiences that promote engagement.

Cross-racial interaction is a key form of student engagement that has been shown by a large number of independent studies to have a significant positive effect on a range of educational outcomes. In *Making Diversity Work on Campus,* we noted strong evidence that the frequency of cross-racial interaction that occurs during the normal course of undergraduate life contributes in positive ways to students' learning and educational experiences. (Other recent studies that were not reviewed in our synthesis also support this claim; see, for example, Hu and Kuh, 2003; Antonio and others, 2004; Zúñiga, Williams, and Berger, 2005). The numerous positive findings not only confirm that exposure and interaction with diverse peers is educationally significant, but they also support a well-established premise regarding student development: that students' interpersonal interactions with peers are one of the most powerful educational resources in higher education.

Gordon Allport (1954) offered perhaps the most widely recognized theory about the benefits and dynamics of cross-racial interaction or contact. He showed through a series of studies that interaction can lead to positive outcomes; however, the benefits are contingent on the presence of appropriate conditions. Without certain conditions in place, contact may even heighten rather than reduce racial prejudice. According to Allport's well-known intergroup contact theory, cross-racial interaction is more likely to lead to positive race relations when it occurs under equal group status within the situation, pursuit of common goals, intergroup cooperation, and the support of authorities, law, or custom. A sizable body of research has since extended and clarified the conditions that are likely to improve the quality and results of cross-racial interaction (see Pettigrew, 1998, for a review). In short, contact theory makes clear that if positive results from cross-racial interaction are desired, the environmental conditions that improve the quality of contact are just as important as having the interpersonal contact.

Nonracist Cultures, Milieu, and Cross-Racial Interactions

Although the benefits of cross-racial interaction have been examined broadly and systematically within the study of higher education, the equally important campus conditions that support higher levels of interaction and presumably more positive contact have been understudied. However, in our 2004 study, Alexander W. Astin, Dongbin Kim, and I found that some of the ideal conditions for improving cross-racial interaction include a more racially diverse student body and more opportunities for students to live and work on campus. Although the intergroup contact theory was not actually tested, the findings in our study as well as those of others (Pike and Kuh, 2006; Umbach and Kuh, 2006) support the notion that environmental conditions do matter in determining the frequency of contact found in colleges and universities.

Although identifying the full range of specific conditions is important, this process may not necessarily capture the more fundamental issues, institutional culture, and milieu that are linked to the core of a campus. These issues are much more difficult to specify. According to some scholars (Smith and others, 1997; Hurtado, Milem, Clayton-Pedersen, and Allen, 1998), the successful implementation of those ideal conditions for cultivating positive cross-racial interactions is inextricably linked to establishing a nonracist culture or climate, which includes altering the legacy of exclusion, revamping organizational structure, and seriously rethinking the psychological and behavioral climate of the campus. Although there has been serious contemplation about what a nonracist culture or climate might look like in higher education (see, for example, Hale, 2004), there is no consensus regarding exactly what institutions must do to achieve this type of environment.

Part of the reason for this lack of consensus is that each college or university faces a set of unique circumstances that cannot be easily addressed by ready-made cookbook strategies. Richardson and Skinner (1990), for example, concluded in their study of nine four-year institutions that the coordination of a wide variety of strategies is more critical than the implementation of a particular program or policy for determining the success of how institutions adapt successfully to diversity. Nevertheless, arguments pointing to the importance of addressing race in campus cultures and climates suggest that a superficial accounting of specific conditions, programs, or policies fails to fully describe the complex dynamics and qualities of a college or university that sustains positive cross-racial interactions among students.

If there is indeed a unique dynamic or quality linked to a set of conditions associated with positive cross-racial interactions, which is presumably just as important as having interpersonal contact, then it stands to reason that this type of environment should have a unique effect on student outcomes that extends beyond a student's own level of cross-racial interaction. In other words, students should uniquely benefit not only from their own interactions with someone of a different race or ethnicity, but also from being enrolled in an institution that sustains positive race relations, since one's own individual interactions are distinct from the institutional context in which they occur. In a recent study, colleagues and I found that students who have very little cross-racial interaction yet are part of a student body that has high average levels of interaction tend to report greater individual gains in their openness to diversity than those who have the same level of interaction but are a part of a student body that has low average levels (Chang, Denson, Sáenz, and Misa, 2006). In other research, Umbach and Kuh (2006) found that institutional support for encouraging contact among students of different economic, social, and racial backgrounds has positive effects on a wide range of educational gains for students at liberal arts colleges.

Engaging Race in the Absence of Structural Diversity

How might a campus environment that possesses relatively high overall levels of cross-racial contact among students yield unique positive results, independent of a student's own frequency of interaction? Some scholars (Richardson and Skinner, 1990; Smith and others, 1997; Allen and Solórzano, 2001; Hurtado, Dey, Gurin, and Gurin, 2003; Hale, 2004) suspect that campuses with higher levels of cross-racial interaction among the student body have in place a curriculum that reflects the historical and contemporary experiences of people of color; programs that support the recruitment, retention, and graduation of students of color; and an institutional mission that reinforces the colleges' commitment to pluralism. Such campuses might also more carefully and intentionally attend to their historical legacy of exclusion, structural diversity, and student perceptions of racial tension or discrimination (Hurtado, Milem, Clayton-Pedersen, and Allen, 1998).

Whatever the specific conditions might be, students who attend campuses with higher peer average cross-racial interaction levels are not only benefiting from simply observing more students interacting across racial differences, but are likely also benefiting from the overall institutional quality that sustains positive race relations that make higher overall frequency of contact possible. Campuses that actively and intentionally establish the conditions, culture, climate, and dynamic that sustain higher levels of cross-racial interaction among students might be reassured to know that even students who report little or no interaction will also likely benefit from institutional efforts to sustain positive race relations.

Pitfalls of Achieving and Maintaining Positive Race Relations

The research literature suggests that racial diversity can be a powerful tool for adding value to students' educational experiences and learning. There are unfortunately many pitfalls that undermine an institution's capacity to achieve the added educational benefits for students and make a positive difference on the broader race problem in the United States. I briefly highlight some of these. This discussion is primarily intended to raise issues that might help educators think more deeply about their campus efforts.

Artificial Process. It is becoming increasingly clear that the effects of diversity are conditional. In order to understand if diversity matters, we also need to understand what makes diversity work or fall short. However, to answer the what question, particularly to strategize interventions, each institution needs to conduct a serious assessment of its campus, since the challenges for each institution are unique. Although each institution can benefit in planning from large-scale studies that arrive at generalizable conclusions, the details for the actual interventions for any one institution should emerge within it or more organically in a way that engages the most marginalized members on campus. There are certainly good practices, but any listing of interventions for consideration will need to emerge from and be vetted through an organic process of information gathering. The long-term effort to implement the interventions to improve campus racial dynamics and race relations is an organic process carried out by those who know best, the determinant economic, political, ideological, cultural, and social forces driving the relationships among the multiple campus constituencies.

Too often the process of improving the racial dynamics on some campuses and, with it, race relations is experienced as being more artificial than organic. When this occurs, disgruntled or discouraged campus members raise upsetting questions about the motives, decision making, commitment, representation, adequacy of resources, transparency, leadership, and goals associated with those efforts. When it comes to facilitating and sustaining meaningful institutional change, much can be learned from the University of Southern California's Equity Scorecard Project, which Frank Harris III and Estela Mara Bensimon describe in Chapter Six. Although the overarching goal of that project is to achieve equity in educational outcomes, what it takes to achieve that important goal no doubt also benefits campus racial dynamics. That project illustrates the effectiveness of an accountability framework that purposefully moves institutions beyond approaching diversity as simple window dressing.

Uncharacteristic Naiveté. Related to the artificial pursuit of improving how race is experienced on campus is the degree of naiveté associated with sincere efforts to address racial discrimination and prejudice. In the article "Improving Campus Racial Dynamics: A Balancing Act among Competing Interests" (2000), I argued that most institutions indiscriminately mix antiracist endeavors with other institutional interests, failing to examine their impact on one another. No serious consideration is given to how addressing the notion of race as part of institutional life can both expose competition among institutional interests and amplify the tension between them. I argued that when these effects are left unresolved, they not only neutralize diversity-related efforts but also exacerbate intergroup tension. Consequently, even the best-informed and most promising efforts that seek to improve racial dynamics conflict with long-held institutional assumptions, ideals, expectations, values, or practices.

I maintained that when institutions take on matters of race, they should be prepared to experience aggravated tension between competing interests and confront critically long-held assumptions, values, ideals, expectations, and practices. Correspondingly, Alexis de Tocqueville, Gunnar Myrdal, W.E.B. DuBois, and Martin Luther King Jr. have all pointed to the destructive racial circumstances in American society to expose the contradiction between what is supposedly guaranteed by our cherished democratic principles and how these principles are systematically applied and broadly experienced. They keenly observed that the dynamics of race and racism create an irrepressible tension among competing interests, raising the specter of hypocrisy concerning our nation's democratic claims.

Racial Stratification. According to Diamond (2006), Black students face a racialized educational terrain that creates a host of disadvantages for them, which largely explains the achievement gap between Whites and Blacks. He draws from a broad body of research to argue that compared to their White counterparts, Black students are (1) taught by less qualified teachers, (2) concentrated in lower educational tracks, (3) given fewer opportunities to learn because their teachers hold lower expectations of them than other students, (4) attending lower-performing schools at disproportionately higher rates, (5) are more likely to be concentrated in poor households and live in segregated neighborhoods, and (6) face the symbolic costs attached to race, which suggests that Blacks are intellectually inferior to Whites. Much of what Diamond describes also applies with varying degrees to other underrepresented minority groups, such as Latinos and Native Americans.

The achievement gap at the end of high school between underrepresented racial minority students and their White and Asian counterparts contributes not only to whether students go to college but also to where they attend. Trent and his colleagues (2003) show that of those undergraduates within different racial groups, African Americans, Native Americans, and, to a slightly lesser extent, Latinos are underrepresented in the most research-intensive institutions (which include nearly all of the nation's most selective and prestigious universities) compared with Whites and Asian American students. They argue that the different levels of representation found for each racial group in different sectors of U.S. higher education affect the diversity of enrollment patterns.

In short, the opportunities to have sustained and meaningful contact with someone of another racial group in higher education are constrained by racial stratification in the educational system. Significant differences in precollege opportunities contribute not only to whether students from certain racial groups enroll in college but also to where they will likely enroll. When it comes to enrolling more underrepresented racial minority students, many of the nation's most oversubscribed universities face even more difficult challenges because they must contend with racial disparities related to both college-going rates and enrollment patterns across different sectors of higher education.

Policy Barriers. One way to address racial stratification is to have in place state and federal policies as well as institutional practices that level the playing field for underrepresented students. However, the chances of closing educational attainment gaps between racial groups and thereby reducing racial segregation in higher education have been weakened by several policy developments. For example, the weakening of affirmative action, particularly its application to higher education through public referendum and litigation, not only limits the tools universities can use to admit qualified underrepresented minority students but also undermine their capacity to offer attractive financial aid packages for those students. Pusser (2004) studied how the University of California system came to eliminate race-conscious admissions policies during the mid-1990s. He contends that such policy developments encompass far more than the institution itself and unfold in "a dynamic that moves well beyond our understanding of bureaucratic expertise, interest articulation, and organizational culture" (p. 211). Although the process of policymaking is intensely involved and its effects are far reaching, an institution can still play a critical role in the outcome.

Policies that reduce the chances of enrolling a critical mass of underrepresented minority students have a negative impact on the chances that students will have meaningful contact because the racial composition has a significant effect on the probability of having such encounters (Chang, Astin, and Kim, 2004; Pike and Kuh, 2006). If policymaking moves toward reducing educational opportunities for underrepresented minority students, we may be, according to Pusser (2004), "burning down the house." That is, the main structure for achieving equitable access may be dismantled, making it much more difficult to diversify student bodies, which subsequently nullifies the positive educational effects of diversity. As Pusser pointed out, institutions can be much more thoughtful and intentional about preventing their own house from being burned down.

Self-Segregation. The issue of self-segregation and racial balkanization has wrongly focused on students of color. One typical fear has been that as the student body becomes more racially diverse, the campus necessarily becomes more racially divided or balkanized, particularly when there is a proliferation of student clubs, as well as curriculum, organized around racial or ethnic groups. Research, however, does not seem to support this charge, particularly the extent to which this occurs, as suggested by one of my studies (Chang, Astin, and Kim, 2004). We found that students of color show generally higher levels of cross-racial interaction on institutions with greater levels of racial diversity than on those with lower levels.

Perhaps in addition to asking, "Why are all the Black kids sitting together in the cafeteria?" as Tatum (1997) explained so well, we should also be asking, "Why are all the White kids sitting together in the cafeteria?" Indeed, in my study with Astin and Kim (2004), we found that White students are much less likely than students of color to engage in cross-racial interaction. Some of this is due to what has already been discussed: artificial process, institutional naiveté, racial stratification, and policy barriers. There is also the effect of institutional norms, which cannot be detached from an institution's historical development and structures of oppression, which tend to favor White male students. According to some cultural theorists (Bourdieu and Passeron, 1977), when institutions devalue nondominant cultural forms such as those that are common among underrepresented students, it heightens the racialization and politicization of student groups. Under these circumstances, marginalized students will develop oppositional subcultures of resistance, and those privileged by dominant cultural forms will be emboldened by a false sense of superiority, which taken together has a negative effect on both the quantity and quality of cross-racial interactions.

Much attention has focused on oppositional subcultures, but not enough has focused on the extent to which White privilege contributes to so-called self-segregation or balkanization on campus.

Addressing Artificial Integration

The challenges I have discussed are far from a comprehensive inventory or treatment of the many obstacles that educators have to keep in mind when considering interventions geared toward improving campus racial dynamics and race relations. Although there is much more to be said, the purpose of this brief discussion is simply to show the complexity of racial dynamics and the inadequacy of some approaches. Too often, diversity-related efforts emerge out of a knee-jerk reaction to demands from a crisis or from concerned members of the campus community, and there is a failure to see the bigger picture. What subsequently occurs on those campuses is what I call *artificial integration*, where campuses basically fall into the trappings of the pitfalls that I have raised.

To understand the bigger picture, educators ought to consider reimagining what integration or higher levels of cross-racial interaction among a racially diverse student body might ideally look like on their campus. To start off this reimagination that moves campuses away from artificial integration, I offer three related suggestions. First, a reimagined notion of integration should be decoupled from the notion of assimilation, which is how integration has been approached for too long. For example, integration should critically address how the normative culture of an institution affects students' experiences and learning. Comparatively, one major problem with assimilation is that this approach tends to embrace the romanticized norms of a campus culture and its related set of institutional arrangements, which often privileges certain racial groups of students and marginalizes others.

Second, we need to be mindful of the larger racial context in which campus dynamics and interactions take place. When this broader context is taken seriously, it should affect how a campus approaches integration in some important ways. For one, the gaze of integration would be recast on White students since they tend to be the more privileged and are more likely than other groups of students to come from segregated neighborhoods and continue that pattern of segregation as college students (Milem and Umbach, 2003; Sáenz, 2005).

Also, being mindful of context can broaden our understanding that for underrepresented students, organizing around their racial identity and promoting cross-racial interaction are not mutually exclusive efforts but rather can be mutually beneficial given the intractable effects of racism. I have argued that the context for campus racial dynamics has become much more complex, as illustrated by the expansion of student organizations that center on race- or ethnic-based interests (Chang, 2002b). An Asian Pacific American student organization, for example, may offer some students who have just entered college a chance to become engaged through a setting that is less tax-ing for them. As these students spend more time on campus and expand their interests, that initial engagement may provide them the confidence and oppor-tunity through interorganizational collaborations to work or socialize with students of other races. Without such organizations, those students attracted to them may be totally disengaged from campus or even leave, reducing the chances of having meaningful future contact with their undergraduate peers. The bigger point of this example is that race- or ethnic-based student organi-zations that are often considered an obstacle to integration serve multiple pur-poses in the light of a racialized campus context. How they serve participants will vary depending on students' developmental needs during college, which also vary depending on the amount of time they spend on campus.

Third, realizing the educational benefits of diversity is inextricably linked to both targeted interventions on campus and to state and federal policies that remedy the effects of present and past discrimination. In other words, educational interests capitulate to remedial interests, because with-out first addressing racism, the types of educational benefits I referred to at the beginning of this chapter will not emerge from diversity (Chang, Chang, and Ledesma, 2005). In the end, diversity is hard work that provides a means to achieve the greater ends of institutional transformation oriented toward social justice (Chang, 2002a).

In this chapter, I identified some major pitfalls associated with cross-racial interaction on colleges and universities and made suggestions for how campuses can move away from artificial integration toward more promising possibilities. I also draw from the research related to the diversity rationale to make the case that if educators better prepare students to work toward a society that minimizes the types of "crashes" seen in the Oscar-winning movie, there will be an impressive range of positive returns for their stu-dents and for society. Most of my suggestions for how campuses might increase and improve cross-racial engagement have been mostly conceptual or based on the quantitative studies that I know best. William Trent at the University of Illinois once told me that the concept of desegregation tends to focus on demographic changes, which is easier to assess quantitatively than integration that involves normative changes. Although I have made a big deal about integration, my quantitative orientation limits my capacity to provide more practical implications for normative change.

However, given the practical orientation of this *New Directions* volume, I will overreach slightly and offer a few suggestions to promote the type of integration that I have been advocating. Most of what I briefly point out is anecdotal, based on my own varied professional work over the years, so what follows should be considered with this in mind. First, institutions should have in place mechanisms that seek to achieve three core purposes: the detection, correction, and prevention of discrimination. These mechanisms are essential for any campus serious about addressing diversity because they address the most fundamental obstacles for positive race relations. Second, campuses should cultivate a willingness among its members to have difficult conversations about conflicting beliefs and values, lead in courageous and committed ways, put into question cherished beliefs, confront institutional shortcomings, make hard compromises, resist moral panic, refrain from demonizing opposing positions, build trust, renegotiate constantly (particularly power), and address the intentional or unintentional privileging of learning that may have disproportionately negative consequences on certain groups. These are broader aspects of a campus that I have come to appreciate better through personal observations and conversations and that are better suited for qualitative inquiry, so I will refrain from saying any more about them.

What is listed above lacks necessary details. In the end, however, each campus will need to fill in the finer details through an organic process. What I have raised so far is mainly a starting point for the much more demanding work of planning and then executing campus integration. When campuses do that work well, the potential benefits are appropriately documented. When they fail to do it at all, Harvard Law School professor Lani Guinier (2003) suggested that the immediate and long-term societal costs are unmistakably high.

References

Allen, W. R., and Solórzano, D. G. "Affirmative Action, Educational Equity and Campus Racial Climate: A Case Study of the University of Michigan Law School." *La Raza Law Journal*, 2001, *12*, 237–363.

Allport, G. *The Nature of Prejudice*. Reading, Mass.: Addison-Wesley, 1954.

Antonio, A. L., and others. "Effects of Racial Diversity on Complex Thinking in College Students." *Psychological Science*, 2004, *15*(8), 507–510.

Bakke v. *Regents of the University of California*, 553 P.2d 1152 (Cal. 1976).

Bourdieu, P., and Passeron, J. *Reproduction in Education, Society and Culture*. Thousand Oaks, Calif.: Sage, 1977.

Chang, M. J. "Improving Campus Racial Dynamics: A Balancing Act Among Competing Interests." *Review of Higher Education*, 2000, *23*(2), 153–175.

Chang, M. J. "Preservation or Transformation: Where's the Real Educational Discourse on Diversity?" *Review of Higher Education*, 2002a, *25*(2), 125–140.

Chang, M. J. "Racial Dynamics on Campus: What Student Organizations Can Tell Us." *About Campus*, 2002b, *7*(1), 2–8.

Chang, M. J. "Reconsidering the Diversity Rationale." *Liberal Education*, 2005, *91*(1), 6–13.

Chang, M. J., Astin, A. W., and Kim, D. "Cross-Racial Interaction Among Undergraduates: Some Causes and Consequences." *Research in Higher Education*, 2004, *45*(5), 527–551.

Chang, M. J., Chang, J., and Ledesma, M. C. "Beyond Magical Thinking: Doing the Real Work of Diversifying Our Institutions." *About Campus*, 2005, *10*(2), 9–16.

Chang, M. J., Denson, N., Sáenz, V., and Misa, K. "The Educational Benefits of Sustaining Cross-Racial Interaction Among Undergraduates." *Journal of Higher Education*, 2006, *77*(3), 430–455.

Chang, M. J., Witt, D., Jones, J., and Hakuta, K. (eds.). *Compelling Interest: Examining the Evidence on Racial Dynamics in Colleges and Universities*. Stanford, Calif.: Stanford University Press, 2003.

Diamond, J. B. "Are We Barking Up the Wrong Tree? Rethinking Oppositional Culture Explanations for the Black/White Achievement Gap." Unpublished manuscript, 2006.

DuBois, W.E.B. *Souls of Black Folk: Essays and Sketches*. Chicago: A. C. McClung, 1903.

Gratz v. *Bollinger,* 123 2411 (S. Ct. 2003).
Grutter v. *Bollinger,* 124 35 (S. Ct. 2003).
Guinier, L. "Admissions Rituals as Political Acts: Guardians at the Gates of Our Democratic Ideals." *Harvard Law Review,* 2003, *117,* 113.
Hale, F. W. (ed.). *What Makes Racial Diversity Work in Higher Education: Academic Leaders Present Successful Policies and Strategies.* Sterling, Va.: Stylus, 2004.
Hu, S., and Kuh, G. D. "Diversity Experiences and College Student Learning and Personal Development." *Journal of College Student Development,* 2003, *44*(3), 320–334.
Hurtado, S., Dey, E. L., Gurin, P., and Gurin, G. "College Environments, Diversity, and Student Learning." In J. C. Smart (ed.), *Higher Education: Handbook of Theory and Research.* New York: Kluwer, 2003.
Hurtado, S., Milem, J. F, Clayton-Pedersen, A., and Allen, W. R. "Enhancing Campus Climates for Racial/Ethnic Diversity: Educational Policy and Practice." *Review of Higher Education,* 1998, *21*(3), 279–302.
Milem, J. F., Chang, M. J., and Antonio, A. L. *Making Diversity Work on Campus: A Research-Based Perspective.* Washington, D.C.: American Association of Colleges and Universities, 2005.
Milem, J. F., and Umbach, P. D. "The Influence of Precollege Factors on Students' Predispositions Regarding Diversity Activities in College." *Journal of College Student Development,* 2003, *44*(5), 611–624.
Moses, M. S., and Chang, M. J. "Toward a Deeper Understanding of the Diversity Rationale." *Educational Researcher,* 2006, *35*(1), 6–11.
Pettigrew, T. "Intergroup Contact Theory." *Annual Review of Psychology,* 1998, *49,* 65–85.
Pike, G. R., and Kuh, G. D. "Relationships Among Structural Diversity, Informal Peer Interaction, and Perception of the Campus Environment." *Review of Higher Education,* 2006, *29*(4), 425–450.
Pusser, B. *Burning Down the House: Politics, Governance, and Affirmative Action at the University of California.* Albany: State University of New York Press, 2004.
Richardson, R. C., and Skinner, E. F. "Adapting to Diversity: Organizational Influences on Student Achievement." *Journal of Higher Education,* 1990, *61*(5), 485–511.
Sáenz, V. B. "Breaking the Cycle of Segregation: Examining Students' Pre-College Racial Environments and Their Diversity Experiences in College." Unpublished doctoral dissertation, University of California, Los Angeles, 2005.
Smith, D. G., and others. *Diversity Works: The Emerging Picture of How Students Benefit.* Washington, D.C.: Association of American Colleges and Universities, 1997.
Tatum, B. D. *Why Are All the Black Kids Sitting Together in the Cafeteria?* New York: Basic Books, 1997.
Trent, W., and others. "Justice, Equality of Educational Opportunity and Affirmative Action in Higher Education." In M. J. Chang, D. Witt, J. Jones, and K. Hakuta (eds.), *Compelling Interests: Examining the Evidence on Racial Dynamics in Colleges and Universities.* Stanford, Calif.: Stanford University Press, 2003.
Umbach, P. D., and Kuh, G. D. "Student Experiences with Diversity at Liberal Arts Colleges: Another Claim for Distinctiveness." *Journal of Higher Education,* 2006, *77*(1), 169–192.
Zúñiga, X., Williams, E. A., and Berger, J. B. "Action-Oriented Democratic Outcomes: The Impact of Student Involvement with Campus Diversity." *Journal of College Student Development,* 2005, *46*(6), 660–678.

MITCHELL J. CHANG is associate professor of higher education and organizational change at the University of California, Los Angeles.

NEW DIRECTIONS FOR STUDENT SERVICES • DOI: 10.1002/ss

3

In this chapter, the use of theory and its role in understanding racial realities are addressed through a critical race theory lens. The chapter offers recommendations for creating and applying theoretical race perspectives in higher education and student affairs.

Critical Race Perspectives on Theory in Student Affairs

Lori D. Patton, Marylu McEwen, Laura Rendón, Mary F. Howard-Hamilton

Student development theory has been used to make sense of attitudes, behaviors, norms, and outcomes among college students since the late 1970s. In addition, educators, administrators, and researchers rely on theories of retention and student success, organizational development, learning, and campus environments in their efforts to understand diverse groups of students (McEwen, 2003, Torres, Howard-Hamilton, and Cooper, 2003). Although these theories contribute substantially to higher education and student affairs work, they are limited in their use of language about race and considerations of the roles of racism in students' development and learning.

The purpose of this chapter is threefold. First, we highlight the value, role, and uses of theory in higher education and student affairs, as well as the omission of race, racism, and racial realities in the theories commonly used in the profession. Second, we introduce critical race theory as a framework for not only understanding our use of theories but also for guiding practice on college and university campuses. Third, we address the intersection of race with other identities (Jones and McEwen, 2000; Abes, Jones, and McEwen, 2007; Robinson and Howard-Hamilton, 2000) and offer recommendations for practice.

NEW DIRECTIONS FOR STUDENT SERVICES, no. 120, Winter 2007 © Wiley Periodicals, Inc.
Published online in Wiley InterScience (www.interscience.wiley.com) • DOI: 10.1002/ss.256

The Role of Theory in Student Affairs

Theory provides a strong basis for knowledge, expertise, and practice and serves as a foundation for the student affairs profession (McEwen, 2003). Without theory, professionals may informally attempt to make sense of observations and phenomena. However, this version of sense making tends to be less cohesive and less consistent than theory-based approaches to understanding students. Theories provide an overarching perspective about a certain trend or set of phenomena. Moreover, they offer ways to communicate about students among other professionals and provide a "common language" within a "community of scholars" (Knefelkamp, 1982, p. 380) that enables educators to talk with students about salient developmental issues.

In addition to providing a foundation for practice, theories help professionals consider the relationships among elements we observe and often serve "to simplify the complex—to connect what appears to be random and to organize what appears to be chaotic" (McEwen, 2003, p. 154). Theory by its very nature tends to be reductionistic, as it focuses on specific dimensions of a set of phenomena and how these dimensions fit together into an integrated and complex whole. Professionals rely on theory "to make the many complex facets of experience manageable, understandable, meaningful, and consistent rather than random" (McEwen, 2003, p. 154). Overall, however, race, racism, and racial realities have been generally ignored among the interrelationships and phenomena incorporated in theories pertaining to students and their development (Torres, Howard-Hamilton, and Cooper, 2003).

Although some developmental theories were introduced in the 1950s and 1960s (for example, Chickering, 1969; Heath, 1968; Heath, 1964; Perry, 1970; Sanford, 1962, 1967), it was not until the late 1970s, with the publication of Knefelkamp, Widick, and Parker's *Applying New Developmental Findings* (1978), that student development became central to the student affairs profession. In the 1970s, models of Black identity development emerged (Cross, 1971), along with models of sexual identity development (Cass, 1979) and minority identity development (Atkinson, Morten, and Sue, 1979). Others emerged in the 1980s and 1990s pertaining to race (Cross, 1991, 1995; Cross and Fhagen-Smith, 2001; Hardiman, 2001; Helms, 1995; Helms and Cook, 1999; Horse, 2001), sexual orientation (D'Augelli, 1994; Fassinger and Miller, 1997; McCarn and Fassinger, 1996), and gender (Downing and Roush, 1985; Osanna, Helms, and Leonard, 1992). A wide array of theories, some new and updated, are now available to address psychosocial development (Chickering and Reisser, 1993), intellectual development (Baxter Magolda, 1992), McCarn and Fassinger, 1996), multiple dimensions of identity (Jones and McEwen, 2000; Abes, Jones, and McEwen, 2007), multiple oppressions (Reynolds and Pope, 1991), self-authorship (Baxter Magolda, 2001), and mixed-race students (Renn, 2004). Notwithstanding, classic theories offered by Chickering (1969), Perry (1970, 1981), Kohlberg (1975), and Tinto (1975, 1993) remain among the most frequently cited.

NEW DIRECTIONS FOR STUDENT SERVICES • DOI: 10.1002/ss

What has been lacking in the knowledge and use of theory by higher education and student affairs professionals is a critical examination of theories: the research base, the perspective of the theorists, the research generated, and how theories evolve. Furthermore, the teaching of theory in graduate preparation programs is mostly focused on knowing the theories and their various stages. It is also important, however, that educators using a theory know themselves and recognize how their lenses or perspectives inform their interpretations and critiques. In order to use theory to inform and then transform practice, as Hall suggested (cited in Apple, 1993), it is essential that higher education and student affairs professionals engage in a critical examination of theories and of themselves as users of theory. One such way is through exploring the often disregarded roles of race and racism.

Racelessness in Student Development Theory

Unfortunately, except for racial identity development theories and race as one social identity in Jones and McEwen's (2000) and Abes, Jones, and McEwen's (2007) models of multiple identities, little attention has been devoted to incorporating race into the theories most widely used in the profession. In fact, many seem to replicate Erikson's (1968) minimal and patronizing attention to race in his characterization of the lost, confused, and "surrendered identity" contained in the writings of Black authors such as W.E.B. DuBois, James Baldwin, and Ralph Ellison. Although it is noteworthy that Erikson wrote an entire chapter in his book on the identities of Black Americans, his writings clearly indicate a struggle with how race related to identity, and the chapter comes across as presenting African Americans as developmentally deficient. Most student affairs educators are probably more familiar with Erikson's life span theory of human development and have not been exposed to what he wrote about the identity of African Americans. This is somewhat ironic given that many theories used today, particularly psychosocial, are grounded in Erikson's work.

Let us briefly examine a sample of three theories in student development and how race and racism were ignored by the theorists. Chickering and Reisser (1993) offered a revision of Chickering's original model (1969). Although Chickering and Reisser state that "reflecting on one's family of origin and ethnic heritage" (p. 49) is one part of developing identity and references are made to Cross's Black racial identity model (1971) and Atkinson, Morten, and Sue's minority identity model (1983), Chickering and Reisser do not directly discuss race and racism and how they may influence identity development. Furthermore, they offer no discussion of how race and racism may intersect with the seven vectors, even though racial identity development theory, research on racial identities, and research about the psychological aspects of racism were available in the literature when their revised model was published.

In a second example, Baxter Magolda (1992) has contributed significantly to research and literature with her model of the epistemological development of college students. However, she indicated that only 3 of the 101 students in her original study were from "nondominant populations" and that all three students from "underrepresented groups" "were unreachable by Year 10 [of her study] due to changing addresses" (Baxter Magolda, 2001, p. 342). Thus, participants remain racially homogeneous in Baxter Magolda's longitudinal study (1992, 2001) of epistemological development and self-authorship.

In a third example, Kohlberg (1975) is credited with creating a theory of moral development and reasoning. The theory has six stages through which individuals move toward reaching a universal level of moral reasoning. Kohlberg acknowledged justice and autonomy as key values that guide moral development but did not account for racial or cultural experiences of people of color in his theory. And there is no indication that he considered the role of race in how societal laws and rules are established, who shapes these decisions, and how people of color might negatively interpret or be affected by such decisions. Consequently, there is little discourse on the experiences of students of color, the moral dilemmas they face in responding to institutional structures constructed by race, or the implications of these dilemmas in their moral development.

Illuminating Racial Omissions in Theory

To examine the role of race in theories, several strategies should be used. First, one should consider the base for a theory: (1) whether the theory is empirical; (2) if the theory is empirical, what is known about the participants in the study (or studies) on which the theory is based; and (3) what is known about the theorist, including assumptions informed by her or his academic background and race/ethnicity. Second, the roles of race and racism, as well as power and privilege, within a theory should be considered (Brown, Hinton, and Howard-Hamilton, 2007). Another strategy is to engage in research to examine how well a theory applies to the experiences of a specific racial group of students (Howard-Hamilton, 1997).

Another means of compensating for the omission or minimal attention to race and racism in contemporary theories is through research studies that examine the intersection of one or more of the theories with race and racial identity (Torres, Howard-Hamilton, and Cooper, 2003). Several studies have focused on the intersection of psychosocial development and racial identity for students of different races (Pope, 1998, 2000; Taub, 1995, 1997; Taub and McEwen, 1991, 1992). In their 2004 qualitative study, Torres and Baxter Magolda addressed the role of cognitive development in the ethnic identity development of Latino college students.

A fifth strategy is to examine the theoretical and research literature to develop models that more effectively address race and racism in student development. Two examples exist related to psychosocial theory. For exam-

NEW DIRECTIONS FOR STUDENT SERVICES • DOI: 10.1002/ss

ple, McEwen, Roper, Bryant, and Langa (1990) critiqued the appropriateness of Chickering's theory for African American students. In response, they identified nine additional psychosocial tasks that had been previously overlooked, including developing spiritually, developing racial identity, and developing social responsibility. In another example, Kodama, McEwen, Liang, and Lee (2001, 2002) identified psychosocial issues for Asian American students and offered a modification of Chickering's model, taking into account racism, Asian cultural values, and research about Asian American college students. Howard-Hamilton (1997, 2003) connected student development theories and the social learning model to identity issues that African American women and men face. In addition to these approaches, a critical race perspective is warranted and explained more fully in the next section.

Race-Based Theories and Their Applicability in Higher Education

A critical race perspective entails recognition that racism is a normal and common aspect that shapes society. Race is deeply embedded in social, cultural, and political structures, thus making it difficult to recognize and address (Delgado and Stefancic, 2001; Ladson-Billings, 1999). Furthermore, race is socially constructed, with historical interpretations that marginalize people of color (Morfin and others, 2006). Another assumption is that the voices and experiences of people of color are central, legitimate, and relevant in contexualizing race and racial realities (Solórzano, 1998). Such voices serve as counterstories that challenge universality and conventional interpretations of the educational experience. Also, color-blind racism and racial indifference must consistently be challenged through exposing the manner in which racial advances often come at the cost of promoting or feeding into White self-interests. Forman (2004) noted that color-blind ideologies ignore the systemic nature of race, excuse accountability for racial injustices, and promote apathetic, covert acts of racism, which ultimately place power and privilege with the dominant group.

In 1999, Gloria Ladson-Billings argued that critical race theory (CRT) could be helpful in "unmasking and exposing racism in its various permutations" (p. 12) within education. This strategy should be applied to student development theories and other theoretical models used to inform practice and research in higher education. In this section, we introduce CRT as a framework in which issues of race and social and educational inequities are foregrounded. CRT was created by Black, Latino, and Asian legal scholars as they sought to better understand societal issues such as the failure of civil rights legislation and the relationship between race and the law. Taylor (2000) indicated that CRT has been extended to apply not only to legal issues but also to areas in education and women's studies. CRT is interdisciplinary in its approach because it incorporates various intellectual traditions that promote racial justice (Lawrence, Matsuda, Delgado, and

NEW DIRECTIONS FOR STUDENT SERVICES • DOI: 10.1002/ss

Crenshaw, 1993) and includes an activist dimension that makes known how society is organized around race in order to transform structures that have long perpetuated racial injustice (Delgado and Stefanic, 1999; Solórzano, Villalpando and Oseguera, 2005). As such, elements of CRT could be employed in higher education and student affairs to illuminate racial inequities and hierarchies and to transform colleges and universities.

Ladson-Billings and Tate (1995) introduced the critical race theory of education, which seeks to create a critical perspective that is analogous to that of CRT in the legal arena. Although some might suggest that feminist and class theories have been and could continue to be employed to highlight gender and racial inequities, Ladson-Billings and Tate underscore that race continues to be undertheorized and underused as a mode for understanding educational inequality. Furthermore, they point out that class- and gender-based theories are useful only to a point and are unable to account for all differences in educational achievement. They conceptualize a critical race theory of education with three propositions:

1. Race continues to be a significant factor in determining inequity in the United States.
2. U.S. society is based on property rights.
3. The intersection of race and property creates an analytical tool through which inequities can be understood.

Race and the Maintenance of Educational Inequities. Under the first proposition, Ladson-Billings and Tate argue that race continues to be a significant factor in producing inequities in society and educational institutions. For example, it has been well documented that the educational achievement of students of color lags behind that of their White counterparts. Low-income students of color are more likely to drop out of high school, be suspended, or be incarcerated. They are also more likely to attend resource-poor schools, tracked away from academic programs that lead to college, and placed in vocational programs. Accordingly, students of color often have difficulties enrolling in college because of previous deficiencies created by an educational system where inequities between the rich and the poor persist (Gándara, 2005; Rendón, Garcia, and Person, 2004).

How is this first proposition related to student affairs and services in higher education? It is important for educators and administrators on college and university campuses to understand how race produces inequities. For example, racism could be said to be at the core of a curriculum that focuses exclusively on White, Western viewpoints that render students of color invisible in what is learned and discussed in class. This is particularly true of the many developmental theories that are used in student affairs and higher education graduate programs. For example, in a graduate course on environmental theory, students should be engaged in conversations that allow them to critically examine how students of color experience the var-

NEW DIRECTIONS FOR STUDENT SERVICES • DOI: 10.1002/ss

ious aspects of campus environments (physical, constructed, organizational, human aggregate) and the implications these experiences have for student success. The phrase "theory to practice" is frequently promoted as a method of encouraging students to use theory to guide practice. However, if the theories that guide practice fail to take race into consideration, a huge disservice is ultimately done to the racially diverse student populations with whom future professionals will work.

As Harper and Hurtado note in Chapter One of this volume, race is also an issue in institutions where students of color are significantly underrepresented because they often experience isolation and marginalization. Race is especially evident when students of color experience cultural assaults such as discrimination and stereotyping. Solórzano, Ceja, and Yosso (2000) described such assaults as "racial microaggressions" or "subtle insults (verbal, nonverbal, and/or visual) directed toward people of color, often automatically or unconsciously" (p. 60). Race is also a reality when students of color do not feel safe, welcome, or comfortable in an institutional environment that marginalizes them.

What this means is that in order to transform higher education, student affairs and higher education programs and professionals should incorporate an inclusive curriculum that incorporates a dialogue of race. Ethnic culture centers could also be offered as places where students from specific racial groups can meet, share strategies for resistance, and form communities (Rendón, Garcia, and Person, 2004). These centers might also be viewed as counterspaces where students can retreat from harsh campus racial climates and microaggressions, that is, subtle verbal, nonverbal, or visual insults (Patton, 2006).

Race and Property Rights on College Campuses. Under the second proposition, that U.S. society is based on property rights, Ladson-Billings and Tate (1995) indicate that the history of the United States is replete with examples of tensions and struggles over property: acquiring land belonging to American Indians and Mexicans, viewing Africans as property, and the concept of possessing one's own property, for example. As such, social benefits are placed in the hands of property owners.

Higher education administrators and student affairs educators who use a critical race lens should be cognizant that property differences manifest themselves in various ways on college and university campuses. For example, professors "own" the curriculum in their classrooms and design it according to their own ontological and epistemological assumptions, which may work against students of color. Some faculty subscribe to monocultural, color-blind paradigms that validate Western structures of knowledge: individual achievement, rationality, exclusivity, and the subjugation of knowledge created by indigenous people and people of color. An African American or Latino faculty member with a social justice philosophy is likely to teach U.S. history in a very different way from a White colleague who is not interested in or knowledgeable about issues of race.

NEW DIRECTIONS FOR STUDENT SERVICES • DOI: 10.1002/ss

There are also racial inequities that cannot be ignored with regard to institutional leadership (King and Howard-Hamilton, 2003). For instance, whoever is in power on the college campus "owns" the right to make final decisions and move the institution in a particular way. Women and people of color often possess limited power on many campuses. Although they may be more represented in student affairs divisions, the greatest political power for the most part continues to reside in academic affairs, where fewer women and people of color are found. Faculty and academic administrators such as provosts, vice presidents of academic affairs, deans of academic units, and department chairs are typically considered more politically influential than their colleagues in student affairs. As such, tensions between student and academic affairs exist.

A new vision of institutional leadership should focus on finding the connections that exist between both units and distributing power and influence more equitably across university organizational structures. It is also important to note that issues related to organizational leadership are often addressed in graduate preparation program courses. Thus, faculty who use a critical race perspective can engage newcomers to the profession in a way that challenges them to think about the ways race and racism are embedded in the organization and functions of higher education.

Understanding White Property, Privilege, and Advantage. In the third proposition, the intersection of race and property as a tool for understanding inequity, Ladson-Billings and Tate (1995) contend that the "construction of Whiteness as the ultimate property" (p. 58) is essentially what is most harmful to racial minorities. Accordingly, this notion legitimizes the idea that only what Whites own is "real property." This includes rights to dispose of property; rights to use and enjoy property, reputational, and status capital; and rights to exclude. In education, Ladson-Billings and Tate contended that White property is legitimized when students are rewarded for conformity to White norms, such as speech patterns, dress, and behaviors. Moreover, the nation's most affluent schools are located in predominantly White communities, where children enjoy privileges such as better libraries, exemplary teachers, smaller classes, a fuller range of college-prep courses, and well-trained counselors who know how to get students into college. Whites can also be confident that their identities normally carry more prestige and that they will be not be embarrassed for speaking English, "their language." The White right to exclude is exemplified in the creation and maintenance of separate schools for Whites and Blacks and by resegregation through tracking (that is, placing Black and Hispanic youth in nonacademic programs of study that do not lead to college).

In the light of Ladson-Billings and Tate's third proposition, higher education and student affairs professionals using a critical race perspective should understand that in the college setting, Whites are given agency in a number of ways. For example, the fact that the overwhelming majority of college faculty and senior academic administrators such as presidents, provosts, vice presidents, and deans are White translates to the notion that being White carries more status and power than being of color. When students of color sit together in the cafeteria or in the library, they are usually viewed as segregating themselves, while Whites who exhibit this behavior are considered to be hanging out with their friends (Tatum, 1997). Moreover, students of color who dress with clothes representing their culture and speak a language other than English could experience cultural assaults in the form of discrimination and stereotypes.

It is essential that educators and administrators become more cognizant of the numerous ways in which the experiences, languages, and cultures of students of color are minimized in higher education and seek to transform perceptions, practices, and policies that privilege some students at the expense of others. A critical race lens should also be demonstrated in the preparation of new professionals to help them understand the complex dynamics of how race is constructed to grant agency to one group while disadvantaging and stifling the progress of another.

Intersections of Race and Other Social Identities

Thus far, this chapter has highlighted theory and the importance of recognizing race in the use of theory. In addition to being used as a lens to understand race and issues of racism that are relevant in student affairs practice and the preparation of newcomers to the profession, CRT can be expanded to understand the intersections of multiple social identities. According to Delgado and Stefancic (2001), "intersections" in this context refers to "the examination of race, sex, class, national origin, and sexual orientation, and how their combination plays out in various settings" (p. 51). We add that identities focusing on culture, ethnicity, ability, religion, and faith also are important aspects that must be considered in the multifaceted identities that comprise student populations (Robinson and Howard-Hamilton, 2000). Higher education and student affairs professionals should be knowledgeable about and aware of how their own racial identities influence their decisions and interactions with others (King and Howard-Hamilton, 2003). An awareness of their attitudes toward diversity and multiple identities can empower or thwart the developmental experiences of the students they encounter. Not adhering to the dominant value structure and embracing the critical race theoretical perspective is an important step in creating spaces for safe dialogue, reducing microaggressions on campus, and moving one step further toward understanding the intricacies of multiple identities, including race.

It is important to recognize the multiple identities that make up one's entire persona. Specifically, addressing issues of race only and ignoring the fact that an individual is a woman, lesbian, and from a low socioeconomic status is oppressive because parts of her are pushed to the margins. As Crenshaw (1995) stated, "Ignoring differences within groups contributes to tension among groups" (p. 357). Therefore, it is important to expand the critical race framework to include the intersections of race, gender, sexual orientation, and other characteristics deemed salient by each individual.

The concept of salience is defined as the degree of significance that race or racial identity has in a person's approach to life, which can range from low to high in importance (Vandiver, 2001). Therefore, seeing an African American woman from a unitary lens of race only, and not taking into account gender or class, "obscures the identities and submerges the perspectives of women who differ from the norm" (Delgado, 2000, p. 253). If the multiple identities are nullified, a microaggression has occurred, which is antithetical to the critical race theoretical framework. That is why the concept of intersectionality has been introduced in CRT to explain the convergence of race, gender, class, and sexual orientation and the hidden implications regarding interconnecting forms of social oppression (Su and Yamamoto, 2002). When the multiple identities of individuals are recognized and it is understood that salience transcends race, then educators and administrators in higher education can create interventions that are inclusive rather than delimited based on a monolithic perspective of race. For example, a Latina lesbian may not feel that her needs are being met in a counterspace with women who are discussing traditional relationship issues. Thus, an alternative intervention could be a space for LGBT (lesbian, gay, bisexual, and transgender) allies of color to relax, discuss, and share culturally empowering and supportive stories.

CRT moves beyond an individualistic focus, is respectful of the sociopolitical realities of marginalized groups, and does not reinforce the power structures in society. Moving diverse individuals from the margin to the center of discourses, programs, interventions, and theories may create campuses in which everyone feels validated for their differences (hooks, 2000). Advancing dialogues about the multiple dimensions of identities could increase levels of critical consciousness among students of color as well. It is often felt that if there is disagreement within a racial/ethnic group, there would be a disruption of racial bonding and solidarity (hooks, 2000). Through counterstories and a deeper understanding of the intersections of multiple identities, diverse perspectives can be aired for a progressive political struggle that is serious about transformation (hooks, 1990). "Engaging in intellectual exchange where people hear a diversity of viewpoints enables them to witness first hand solidarity that grows stronger in a context of productive critical exchange and confrontation" (hooks, 1990, p. 6).

Recommendations and Conclusions

We conclude with five recommendations that we believe are crucial in guiding higher education and student affairs professionals toward greater recognition, understanding, and action in relation to informing and transforming practice.

First, we encourage educators and administrators to challenge, question, and critique traditional theoretical perspectives. Many of the theories used to guide practice give little, if any, attention to race. Therefore, we must continuously engage in critical examinations that provide an accurate context of the theorists' backgrounds, identities, and assumptions; the population on which the theory was based; how sociopolitical and historical contexts, privilege, and power may have shaped the theory; and the applicability of the theory to various student populations.

Second, we encourage higher education and student affairs professionals to be open to moving beyond the status quo and recognizing the entrenchment of race in educational settings, including programs and services offered through student affairs divisions. Too often professionals perpetuate the status quo, or one group's construction of what is "normal," without having looked more deeply at the role of race. Consistently ignoring race and its systemic complexities further disadvantages students of color. When professionals recognize the complicity of their actions in maintaining campus environments that oppress nondominant populations, they can move toward realizing the goals of social justice.

Roithmayr (1999) asserted, "The classroom—where knowledge is constructed, organized, produced, and distributed—is a central site for the construction of social and racial power" (p. 5). Therefore, our third recommendation is that faculty who teach in higher education and student affairs graduate programs become more knowledgeable and aware of the power of the classroom environment in preparing future professionals. In essence, professors must be cognizant of the factors that guide decisions on the curriculum, particularly what will and will not be taught and how the material will be presented. Faculty should reflect on how often racial perspectives are incorporated into reading materials, class discussions, and assignments. They should be mindful of the roles that race, power, and privilege play in classroom dynamics, particularly in predominantly White settings, where few students of color are represented. Faculty might consider whose voices are heard and valued in the classroom, as well as the ways courses can be restructured to address race and racial realities.

Actively incorporating a critical race perspective in daily practice is our fourth recommendation. In this way, professionals approach their work with an awareness of the existence of race and the different ways that people experience racial realities. They also are clear about the ways in which race continues to produce societal inequities. Last, they understand how the intersection of race with other social identities presents a clearer picture that is necessary for working with individual students.

Our final recommendation is that higher education and student affairs professionals be knowledgeable about and aware of their own racial identities, honestly evaluate themselves in terms of their understanding of race and racism, and recognize how their knowledge, awareness, and racial identity influence their decisions, policies, and interactions with students from diverse backgrounds.

References

Abes, E. S., Jones, S. R., and McEwen, M. K. "Reconceptualizing the Model of Multiple Dimensions of Identity: The Role of Meaning-Making Capacity in the Construction of Multiple Identities." *Journal of College Student Development*, 2007, *48*(1), 1–22.

Apple, M. W. "Constructing the 'Other': Rightist Reconstructions of Common Sense." In C. McCarthy and W. Crichlow (eds.), *Race, Identity, and Representation in Education.* New York: Routledge, 1993.

Atkinson, D. R., Morten, G., and Sue, D. W. *Counseling American Minorities: A Cross-Cultural Perspective.* Dubuque, Iowa: W. C. Brown, 1979.

Atkinson, D. R., Morten, G., and Sue, D. W. *Counseling American Minorities: A Cross-Cultural Perspective.* (2nd ed.) Dubuque, Iowa: W. C. Brown, 1983.

Baxter Magolda, M. B. *Knowing and Reasoning in College: Gender-Related Patterns in Students' Intellectual Development.* San Francisco: Jossey-Bass, 1992.

Baxter Magolda, M. B. *Making Their Own Way: Narratives for Transforming Higher Education to Promote Self-Development.* Sterling, Va.: Stylus, 2001.

Brown, O. G., Hinton, K. G., and Howard-Hamilton, M. F. *Unleashing Suppressed Voices on College Campuses: Diversity Issues in Higher Education.* New York: Peter Lang, 2007.

Cass, V. C. "Homosexual Identity Formation: A Theoretical Model." *Journal of Homosexuality,* 1979, *4,* 219–233.

Chickering, A. W. *Education and Identity.* San Francisco: Jossey-Bass, 1969.

Chickering, A. W., and Reisser, L. *Education and Identity.* (2nd ed.) San Francisco: Jossey-Bass, 1993.

Crenshaw, K. "The Intersection of Race and Gender." In K. Crenshaw, N. Gotanda, G. Peller, and K. Thomas (eds.), *Critical Race Theory: The Key Writings That Formed the Movement.* New York: New Press, 1995.

Cross, W. E., Jr. "The Negro-to-Black Conversion Experience: Toward a Psychology of Black Liberation." *Black World,* 1971, *20*(9), 13–27.

Cross, W. E., Jr. *Shades of Black: Diversity in African-American Identity.* Philadelphia: Temple University Press, 1991.

Cross, W. E., Jr. "The Psychology of Nigrescence: Revising the Cross Model." In J. G. Ponterotto, J. M. Casas, L. A. Suzuki, and C. M. Alexander (eds.), *Handbook of Multicultural Counseling.* Thousand Oaks, Calif.: Sage, 1995.

Cross, W. E., Jr., and Fhagen-Smith, P. "Patterns of African American Identity Development: A Life Span Perspective." In C. L. Wijeyesinghe and B. W. Jackson III (eds.), *New Perspectives on Racial Identity Development: A Theoretical and Practical Anthology.* New York: New York University Press, 2001.

D'Augelli, A. R. "Identity Development and Sexual Orientation: Toward a Model of Lesbian, Gay, and Bisexual Development." In E. J. Trickett, R. J. Watts, and D. Birman (eds.), *Human Diversity: Perspectives on People in Context.* San Francisco: Jossey-Bass, 1994.

Delgado, R. "Rodrigo's Sixth Chronicle: Intersections, Essences, and the Dilemma of Social Reform." In R. Delgado and J. Stefancic (eds.), *Critical Race Theory: The Cutting Edge.* Philadelphia: Temple University Press, 2000.

Delgado, R., and Stefanic, J. (eds.). *Critical Race Theory: The Cutting Edge.* Philadelphia: Temple University Press, 1999.

Delgado, R., and Stefancic, J. *Critical Race Theory: An Introduction.* New York: New York University Press, 2001.

Downing, N. E., and Roush, K. I. "From Passive Acceptance to Active Commitment: A Model of Feminist Identity Development for Women." *Counseling Psychologist,* 1985, *13,* 695–709.

Erikson, E. H. *Identity: Youth and Crisis.* New York: Norton, 1968.

Fassinger, R. E., and Miller, B. A. "Validation of an Inclusive Model of Homosexual Identity Formation in a Sample of Gay Men." *Journal of Homosexuality,* 1997, *32*(2), 53–78.

Forman, T. A. "Color-Blind Racism and Racial Indifference: The Role of Racial Apathy in Facilitating Enduring Inequalities." In M. Krysan and A. E. Lewis (eds.), *The Changing Terrain of Race and Ethnicity.* New York: Russell Sage Foundation, 2004.

Gándara, P. "Addressing Educational Inequities for Latino Students: The Politics of 'Forgetting.'" *Journal of Hispanic Higher Education,* 2005, 4(3), 295–313.

Hardiman, R. "Reflections on White Identity Development Theory." In C. L. Wijeyesinghe and B. W. Jackson III (eds.), *New Perspectives on Racial Identity Development: A Theoretical and Practical Anthology.* New York: New York University Press, 2001.

Heath, D. H. *Growing Up in College.* San Francisco: Jossey-Bass, 1968.

Heath, R. *The Reasonable Adventurer.* Pittsburgh, Pa.: University of Pittsburgh Press, 1964.

Helms, J. E. "An Update of Helms's White and People of Color Racial Identity Models." In J. G. Ponterotto, J. M. Casas, L. A. Suzuki, and C. M. Alexander (eds.), *Handbook of Multicultural Counseling.* Thousand Oaks, Calif.: Sage, 1995.

Helms, J. E., and Cook, D. A. *Using Race and Culture in Counseling and Psychotherapy: Theory and Process.* Needham Heights, Mass.: Allyn & Bacon, 1999.

hooks, b. *Yearning: Race, Gender, and Cultural Politics.* Boston: South End Press, 1990.

hooks, b. *Feminist Theory: From Margin to Center.* Boston: South End Press, 2000.

Horse, P. G. "Reflections on American Indian Identity." In C. L. Wijeyesinghe and B. W. Jackson III (eds.), *New Perspectives on Racial Identity Development: A Theoretical and Practical Anthology.* New York: New York University Press, 2001.

Howard-Hamilton, M. F. "Theory to Practice: Applying Developmental Theories Relevant to African American Men." In M. J. Cuyjet (ed.), *Helping African American Men Succeed in College.* New Directions for Student Services, no. 80. San Francisco: Jossey-Bass, 1997.

Howard-Hamilton, M. F. (ed.). *Meeting the Needs of African American Women.* New Directions for Student Services, no. 104. San Francisco: Jossey-Bass, 2003.

Jones, S. R., and McEwen, M. K. "A Conceptual Model of Multiple Dimensions of Identity." *Journal of College Student Development,* 2000, 41, 405–414.

King, P. M., and Howard-Hamilton, M. F. "An Assessment of Multicultural Competence." *NASPA Journal,* 2003, 40, 119–133.

King, P. M., and Howard-Hamilton, M. F. "Using Student Development Theory to Inform Institutional Research." In J. W. Pickering and G. R. Hanson (eds.), *Collaboration Between Student Affairs and Institutional Researchers to Improve Institutional Effectiveness.* New Directions for Institutional Research, no. 108. San Francisco: Jossey-Bass, 2001.

Knefelkamp, L. L. "Faculty and Student Development in the '80s: Renewing the Community of Scholars." In H. F. Owens, C. H. Witten, and W. R. Bailey (eds.), *College Student Personnel Administration: An Anthology.* Springfield, Ill.: Thomas, 1982.

Knefelkamp, L. L., Widick, C., and Parker, C. A. (eds.). *Applying New Developmental Findings.* New Directions for Student Services, no. 4. San Francisco: Jossey-Bass, 1978.

Kodama, C. M., McEwen, M. K., Liang, C.T.H., and Lee, S. "A Theoretical Examination of Psychosocial Issues for Asian Pacific American Students." *NASPA Journal,* 2001, 38, 411–437.

Kodama, C. M., McEwen, M. K., Liang, C.T.H., and Lee, S. "An Asian American Perspective on Psychosocial Student Development Theory." In M. K. McEwen and others (eds.), *Working with Asian American College Students.* San Francisco: Jossey-Bass, 2002.

Kohlberg, L. "The Cognitive-Developmental Approach to Moral Education." *Phi Delta Kappan,* 1975, 56, 670–677.

Ladson-Billings, G. "Just What Is Critical Race Theory and What's It Doing in a 'Nice' Field Like Education?" In L. Parker, D. Deyhle, and S. Villenas (eds.), *Race Is . . . Race Isn't: Critical Race Theory and Qualitative Studies in Education.* Boulder, Colo.: Westview Press, 1999.

Ladson-Billings, G., and Tate, W. F. "Toward a Critical Race Theory of Education." *Teachers College Record,* 1995, 97, 47–68.

Lawrence III, C. R., Matsuda, M. J., Delgado, R., and Crenshaw, K. W. "Introduction." In M. J. Matsuda, C. R. Lawrence III, R. Delgado, and K. Crenshaw (eds.), *Words That Wound: Critical Race Theory, Assaultive Speech, and the First Amendment.* Boulder, Colo.: Westview Press, 1993.

McCarn, S. R., and Fassinger, R. E. "Revisioning Sexual Minority Identity Formation: A New Model of Lesbian Identity and Its Implications for Counseling and Research." *Counseling Psychologist,* 1996, *24,* 508–534.

McEwen, M. K. "Nature and Use of Theory." In S. R. Komives and Associates (eds.), *Student Services: A Handbook for the Profession.* (4th ed.) San Francisco: Jossey-Bass, 2003.

McEwen, M. K., Roper, L. D., Bryant, D. R., and Langa, M. "Incorporating the Development of African-American Students into Psychosocial Theories of Student Development." *Journal of College Student Development,* 1990, *31,* 429–436.

Morfin, O. J., and others. "Hiding the Politically Obvious: A Critical Race Theory Preview of Diversity as Racial Neutrality in Higher Education." *Educational Policy,* 2006, *20,* 249–270.

Osanna, S. M., Helms, J. E., and Leonard, M. M. "Do 'Womanist' Identity Attitudes Influence College Women's Self-Esteem and Perceptions of Environmental Bias?" *Journal of Counseling and Development,* 1992, *70,* 402–408.

Patton, L. D. "The Voice of Reason: A Qualitative Examination of Black Student Perceptions of Black Culture Centers." *Journal of College Student Development,* 2006, *47*(6), 628–646.

Perry, W. G., Jr. *Forms of Intellectual and Ethical Development in the College Years: A Scheme.* Troy, Mo.: Holt, Rinehart, and Winston, 1970.

Perry, W. G., Jr. "Cognitive and Ethical Growth: The Making of Meaning." In A. W. Chickering and Associates (eds.), *The Modern American College.* San Francisco: Jossey-Bass, 1981.

Pope, R. L. "The Relationship Between Psychosocial Development and Racial Identity Development of Black College Students." *Journal of College Student Development,* 1998, *39,* 273–282.

Pope, R. L. "The Relationship Between Psychosocial Development and Racial Identity of College Students of Color." *Journal of College Student Development,* 2000, *41,* 302–312.

Rendón, L. I., Garcia, M., and Person, D. *Transforming the First Year of College for Students of Color.* Columbia, S.C.: National Center on the First Year Experience and Students in Transition, 2004.

Renn, K. A. *Mixed Race Students in College: The Ecology of Race, Identity, and Community on Campus.* Albany: State University of New York Press, 2004.

Reynolds, A. L., and Pope, R. L. "The Complexities of Diversity: Exploring Multiple Oppressions." *Journal of Counseling and Development,* 1991, *70,* 174–180.

Robinson, T. L., and Howard-Hamilton, M. F. *The Convergence of Race, Ethnicity, and Gender: Multiple Identities in Counseling.* Columbus, Ohio: Merrill, 2000.

Roithmayr, D. "Introduction to Critical Race Theory in Educational Research and Praxis." In L. Parker, D. Deyle, and S. Villenas (eds.), *Race Is . . . Race Isn't: Critical Race Theory and Qualitative Studies in Education.* Boulder, Colo.: Westview Press, 1999.

Sanford, N. *The American College.* Hoboken, N.J.: Wiley, 1962.

Sanford, N. *Where Colleges Fail: A Study of the Student as a Person.* San Francisco: Jossey-Bass, 1967.

Solórzano, D. G. "Critical Race Theory, Race and Gender Microaggressions, and the Experience of Chicana and Chicano Studies." *International Journal of Qualitative Studies in Education,* 1998, *11,* 121–136.

Solórzano, D. G., Ceja, M., and Yosso, T. "Critical Race Theory, Racial Microaggressions, and Campus Racial Climate: The Experiences of African American College Students." *Journal of Negro Education,* 2000, *69,* 60–73.

Solórzano, D. G., Villalpando, O., and Oseguera, L. "Educational Inequities and Latina/o Undergraduate Students in the United States: A Critical Race Analysis of Their Educational Progress." *Journal of Hispanic Higher Education,* 2005, *4,* 272–294.

Su, J. A., and Yamamoto, E. K. "Critical Coalitions: Theory and Praxis." In F. Valdes, J. McCristal Culp, and A. P. Harris (eds.), *Crossroads, Directions, and a New Critical Race Theory.* Philadelphia: Temple University Press, 2002.

Tatum, B. D. *Why Are All the Black Kids Sitting Together in the Cafeteria? And Other Conversations About Race.* New York: Basic Books, 1997.

Taub, D. J. "Relationship of Selected Factors to Traditional-Age Undergraduate Women's Development of Autonomy." *Journal of College Student Development,* 1995, 36, 141–151.

Taub, D. J. "Autonomy and Parental Attachment in Traditional-Age Undergraduate Women." *Journal of College Student Development,* 1997, 38, 645–654.

Taub, D. J., and McEwen, M. K. "Patterns of Development of Autonomy and Mature Interpersonal Relationships in Black and White Undergraduate Women." *Journal of College Student Development,* 1991, 32, 502–508.

Taub, D. J., and McEwen, M. K. "The Relationship of Racial Identity Attitudes to Autonomy and Mature Interpersonal Relationships in Black and White Undergraduate Women." *Journal of College Student Development,* 1992, 33, 439–446.

Taylor, E. "Critical Race Theory and Interest Convergence in the Backlash Against Affirmative Action: Washington State and Initiative 200." *Teachers College Record,* 2000, 102(3), 538–560.

Tinto, V. "Dropout from Higher Education: A Theoretical Synthesis of Recent Research." *Review of Educational Research,* 1975, 65, 89–125.

Tinto, V. *Leaving College: Rethinking the Causes and Cures of Student Attrition.* (2nd ed.) Chicago: University of Chicago Press, 1993.

Torres, V., and Baxter Magolda, M. "Reconstructing Latino Identity: The Influence of Cognitive Development on the Ethnic Identity Process of Latino Students." *Journal of College Student Development,* 2004, 45, 333–347.

Torres, V., Howard-Hamilton, M. F., and Cooper, D. L. *Identity Development of Diverse Populations: Implications for Teachings and Administration in Higher Education. ASHE-ERIC Higher Education Report* (Vol. 29, No. 6). San Francisco: Jossey-Bass, 2003.

Vandiver, B. J. "Psychological Nigrescence Revisited: Introduction and Overview." *Journal of Multicultural Counseling and Development,* 2001, 29(3), 165–173.

LORI D. PATTON *is assistant professor of higher education in the Department of Educational Leadership and Policy Studies at Iowa State University.*

MARYLU McEWEN *is associate professor emerita in the Department of Counseling and Personnel Services at the University of Maryland, College Park.*

LAURA RENDÓN *is professor of higher education and chair of the Educational Leadership and Policy Studies Department at Iowa State University.*

MARY F. HOWARD-HAMILTON *is professor of higher education at Indiana State University.*

4

Intercultural maturity and the learning partnerships model are offered as frameworks for understanding the intersection of students' developmental levels and readiness for cross-racial interactions, and for assisting educators in promoting racial self-understanding. A case study is used to illustrate the usefulness of the model in supporting student engagement with race.

Enhancing Racial Self-Understanding Through Structured Learning and Reflective Experiences

Stephen John Quaye, Marcia B. Baxter Magolda

Results from a recent campus climate survey at a predominantly White university revealed that students were generally satisfied with their experiences. However, significant differences were discovered when the data were disaggregated by race. While most White students deemed the campus environment welcoming and affirming, several students of color found it hostile, racist, and unreflective of their cultural groups. To better understand how student affairs educators and faculty could improve the campus climate, the dean of students facilitated a series of informal dialogues with leaders of various student organizations on campus. At the initial meeting, six student organization representatives gathered around the table: Jonah (Native American Student Association), Doug (Student Government Association), Kendra (Black Student Alliance), Lester (Asian Student Voices), Rachel (Gamma Nu Omicron, a traditionally White sorority), and Valerie (Latina/o Caucus). The dean encouraged participants to be open in their comments and validated the importance of their voices. Here are excerpts from the dialogue:

JONAH: I don't really understand how the campus feels unwelcoming for Black students. I mean, we celebrated Black History Month a few weeks ago. I remember thinking, "Wow, there are a lot of events going on each day."

NEW DIRECTIONS FOR STUDENT SERVICES, no. 120, Winter 2007 © Wiley Periodicals, Inc.
Published online in Wiley InterScience (www.interscience.wiley.com) • DOI: 10.1002/ss.257

There were tons of speakers, music, and festivals—lots of opportunities for Black students to interact and explore who they are. Native Americans never get that much attention here on campus.

DOUG: I agree with you. And the SGA [Student Government Association] sponsored most of those events. We spent more money on Black History Month than we do recognizing other cultures. I still wonder why we have to hold special celebrations for Blacks. We're all American, and that's what unites us. Focusing on our differences leads to division.

KENDRA: Doug, the problem is that we already celebrate our American heritage all over campus. Have you ever looked at the pictures on the walls of the big room where the SGA meets? Almost all of them are of Whites, which makes us feel that our historical contributions to this university are trivial. I've never once had an African American professor here. I've had to seek out books about my people on my own. These books have helped me think through the racism I experience here and made me more aware of how racism affects other people.

LESTER: Yeah, I remember one day I went to see my calculus professor during office hours because I wasn't doing well in the course. She wondered why I was struggling. Jokingly, she said, "Aren't Asians supposed to be good in math?" Horrified by her comment, I didn't know how to respond, so I just left the office. Before I came here, I enjoyed people's references to how smart I am because I am Asian. Then I started reading the model minority stuff and began to think differently and became offended by those remarks. If there were more Asian people on this campus, my classmates and professors would start to see that we're not all the same.

RACHEL: All of this talk about race is very new to me. My sorority sisters are all White, and we have a good time, and I like all of them. However, I've recently begun to get frustrated by their comments about minorities. They talk about Latinos and African Americans in derogatory ways and don't understand why we need to be more diverse in our recruiting. I feel so alone in the house. While I don't claim to understand minority people's experiences, I'm willing to try and learn.

Following Rachel's comment, the dean recognized visible discomfort among some participants and invited alternative perspectives:

VALERIE: I think the campus climate is fine. I have lots of White friends, and they aren't bad. I think people would be more satisfied with life if they stopped separating themselves from others. I keep telling my friends in the Latino Caucus this, and they just get annoyed with me. I know I'm Latino, but so what? That doesn't mean I have to be segregated from others. Part of the reason I joined the Latino Caucus was to push people to open their eyes and stop dividing themselves. I think the supposedly poor campus climate is the result of minority students purposely excluding themselves from our White friends.

RACHEL: I'm not sure I agree with your point, Valerie. I mean, I never think about my White race inside or outside of class. Most of my friends are White, and all of my teachers are White. I don't understand what it feels like to be a minority person on this campus, but I do think their experiences are different from my own.

DOUG: Oh, come on. All this is nonsense! The university does its best to admit the most qualified students every year. And last year we had a Black person run for SGA president. Doesn't that mean anything?

LESTER: Did that person win? No! That to me means this campus still isn't ready to see students of color in important leadership positions. If anyone besides a White person were in leadership positions in SGA, it would enable us to better understand the experiences of students of color. We need a stronger attention to differences. Right now, there's no attempt by the administration to change the status quo.

KENDRA: Nope, there hasn't been any attempt. There's only so much adjusting to this campus climate that minority students can take. I'm fortunate enough to have my friends in the Black Student Alliance to rely on for support and to recharge after a frustrating day of not hearing about Black people's contributions in my classes. How can other minority people gain an understanding of who they are if there's no exposure to differences in our classes?

JONAH: What frustrates me is the lack of attention to other races as well. You know, just because Native Americans are a very small percentage of the population here doesn't mean our cultural experiences should be ignored. I wish there were more programs for Native Americans here so that we could also explore our heritage.

DOUG: See, there you go again, always focusing on differences. What about our similarities? Why don't we ever focus on that?

After this remark, the dean of students summarized participants' viewpoints and scheduled the next meeting for two weeks later. As Harper and Hurtado note in Chapter One, structured interracial conversations such as this are rare on college campuses. Students struggle with developing an

appreciation for racial diversity and participating in cross-cultural interactions, in large part because they have not developed a strong sense of
their racial identities. This dilemma is exacerbated when educators over-
look the developmental readiness necessary for students to understand
racial differences.

In this chapter, we use intercultural maturity as a framework for understanding students' developmental levels in cross-racial dialogues. We then
illustrate how the learning partnerships model (LPM) (Baxter Magolda,
2004) enables educators to promote racial self-understanding and intercultural maturity among students. We conclude by applying the LPM to the
campus climate meeting to illustrate its usefulness in helping students interact across and learn from racial differences.

Racial Self-Understanding and Intercultural Maturity

For learners to achieve the level of racial understanding that Kendra possesses, educators should devote attention to the holistic development of students. Racial self-understanding evolves through complex development
along three dimensions: (1) cognitive, that is, our beliefs and perspectives
on knowledge, (2) intrapersonal, that is, our sense of self, and (3) interpersonal, that is, our sense of self in relation to others.

King and Baxter Magolda's developmental model of intercultural maturity (2005) is one framework for helping educators envision multiple developmental processes in student learning. Their model depicts students'
initial, intermediate, and mature levels of their own racial self-understanding
and intercultural effectiveness across cognitive, intrapersonal, and interpersonal dimensions. The authors indicate that students who move forward
in their holistic development can more successfully achieve racial self-
understanding and intercultural effectiveness.

In the initial level of development, King and Baxter Magolda note that
students display minimal awareness about their values, racial identities, and
different cultures. Learners here also assume the certainty of knowledge
and form relationships solely with culturally similar peers. The intermediate
level reflects an uncertainty of knowledge and an emerging acknowledgment
of differences. Students also begin to explore their racial identities but refrain
from judging other cultures in cross-racial dialogues. Students at the mature
level of development are able to use multiple cultural frames of reference and
thus can cultivate meaningful relationships with racially diverse persons
and explore the intersections of various social categories. Learners are also
comfortable with their racial identities and actively work to promote social
change within society. Thus, self-authorship, or the internal capacity to gen-
erate one's beliefs, identity, and relationships (Kegan, 1994), is a necessary
developmental foundation for complex racial self-understanding and intercultural maturity (King and Baxter Magolda, 2005).

NEW DIRECTIONS FOR STUDENT SERVICES • DOI: 10.1002/ss

In the student organization meeting, each student reflects a different level of racial self-understanding and intercultural maturity. Doug, Valerie, and Rachel display characteristics associated with the initial level of development. Valerie and Doug do not see themselves as racial beings or understand how their race affects their experiences with their racially diverse peers. They note that a focus on differences divides persons, and they show a lack of consciousness about the problems affecting different racial groups. Although Rachel acknowledges that she does not reflect on her Whiteness, she recognizes that important differences exist between racial groups and wants to begin exploring this area. Jonah and Lester are further along in the exploration process that Rachel desires for herself. They show an intermediate level of understanding about race. Lester's reading of the model minority literature encourages him to question his assumptions about racial differences and his Asian identity. Furthermore, he realizes the significance of racial minority students' attaining prominent leadership positions, as they can offer unique perspectives about the campus climate.

Similarly, Jonah questions the impact that the underrepresentation of Native American students poses on the campus and desperately wants more structured opportunities to explore his racial identity. Finally, Kendra portrays epistemological, intrapersonal, and interpersonal capacities emblematic of an interculturally mature person. Her complex thinking reveals a deep understanding of herself as a Black woman. She seizes opportunities to seek out readings about her racial group on her own and constructs knowledge of how to improve the campus culture for racial minority students. She invites other students into racial dialogues, recognizes that differences do exist, and understands the importance of working to respect and appreciate racial diversity. Moreover, Kendra sees and embraces her role as an active agent for social change.

Illustrating the varying developmental levels of each student clarifies the difficulty in promoting racial self-understanding among developmentally different learners. Students at each level require different support and engagement activities to stimulate their racial development. Unless an educator is cognizant of the developmental foundation necessary for racial self-understanding, a discussion across races can lead learners to reinforce their assumptions rather than interrogate racialized presuppositions, listen to their peers' constructions of race, and collaborate to advance a healthier society rooted in racial justice.

Learning Partnerships: Promoting Racial Self-Understanding and Intercultural Maturity

The Learning Partnerships Model (LPM) (Baxter Magolda, 2004) is a useful framework for promoting self-authorship and intercultural maturity. In this section, we describe the model and provide three examples in which its elements have been applied. Although our particular focus is racial self-understanding, we include examples involving other layers of social identities because they too have utility for promoting racial self-understanding and intercultural maturity. Successful approaches to promoting intercultural maturity share common characteristics. These methods acknowledge learners' racial or social identity development, respect and validate learners' assumptions about their identities and intercultural interactions, invite learners into mutual interactions to explore these notions, and support these explorations to enable more complex perspectives. These characteristics resonate with the core elements of the model.

Learning Partnerships Model. The LPM emerged from Baxter Magolda's longitudinal study (2001) of development among young adults from ages eighteen to thirty-eight. From participants' stories of their educational, employment, and personal experiences that enabled their journeys toward self-authorship during and after college, Baxter Magolda identified six components that balanced respecting learners' present meaning making (support) yet invited them to consider more complex meaning making (challenge). Educators support learners through three principles: validating learners as knowers, situating learning in learners' experiences, and defining learning as mutually constructing meaning. Validating learners as knowers offers recognition for their abilities to develop their own perspectives even when educators may view learners' current perspectives as problematic (as in the dialogue at the outset of this chapter). Situating learning in learners' experiences is crucial to respecting their perspectives and experiences (or lack thereof in the case of intercultural interactions) and enabling them to engage in a serious exploration of those perspectives. Defining learning as mutually constructing meaning offers learners an invitation to construct new meaning collaboratively rather than educators' imposing new perspectives on them. These three supportive principles are central in assisting learners in extracting themselves from the authority dependence most have developed through adolescence and schooling. The principles are particularly important in enabling learners to address the complex process of racial self-understanding despite their inexperience, fear of others' reactions to their beliefs, and perceived threats to their identities.

In addition to the three support principles, educators challenge learners through these assumptions: knowledge is complex and socially constructed, self is central to knowledge construction, and authority and expertise are shared in mutual knowledge construction. Portraying knowledge as complex and socially constructed introduces multiple perspectives and reveals how different vantage points yield diverse perspectives. This depiction also opens the door for viewing oneself as a participant in knowledge construction rather than a recipient of knowledge constructed by authorities. Being aware of the centrality of including self in developing perspectives is reinforced when educators insist that they and their learners share authority and expertise jointly in exploring and crafting more complex perspectives. These challenges are essential in the context of promoting intercultural maturity. The LPM's balance of supportive principles and challenging assumptions is evident, implicitly or explicitly, in the following framework and models of practice to promote social identity development, racial self-understanding, and intercultural effectiveness.

Multicultural Education Framework. Ortiz and Rhoads's multicultural education framework (2000) emphasizes that situating learning in students' experiences is crucial for learning about culture and social justice. This five-step developmental model acknowledges students' initial lack of cultural experience and insufficient awareness of their roles in shaping culture. It also offers a cumulative curriculum for engaging in increasingly complex constructions of racial identity and a multicultural outlook. The first step, understanding culture, engages students in observing and critically analyzing everyday events to understand that culture and people mutually shape each other. Step two, learning about other cultures, invites students to attend cultural events, reflect on their meanings, and talk with persons from diverse backgrounds to understand that cultural groups have deeply rooted values, beliefs, and traditions. In recognizing and deconstructing White culture, step three, students analyze Whiteness to recognize its normalization and question White privilege. This step is a key precursor to helping students recognize the legitimacy of multiple cultures, the goal of step four, in which they identify important aspects of their own cultures and share them with others. Developing a multicultural outlook, step five, engages students in analyzing how institutions shape the expression of culture to help them envision their roles in working toward an equitable society.

The experiential nature of the activities Ortiz and Rhoads (2000) describe—cultural observations and immersions, interactions with diverse others, reflections, and interpretations of one's own culture—situates learning in learners' experiences. These activities, combined with the individual and group reflections on their meanings, validate students as capable of making sense of their experiences. Sharing interpretations of multiple cultural experiences reveals that cultural values and beliefs, including one's own, are complex and socially constructed and that self is central to that process. Mutual sharing of authority and expertise in these dialogues offers respect for students' beliefs and values as they struggle to reconstruct racist assumptions and White privilege to form a multicultural outlook.

Hornak and Ortiz's implementation (2004) of the multicultural education framework in a sixteen-week community college business course revealed the value of the LPM components in helping students develop a multicultural outlook. Despite lack of experience and awareness at the beginning of the course, students made progress in exploring their own pasts and the ideas inherent in their socialization, learning about other cultures, and beginning to understand how culture is created. Owning White privilege, lack of exposure to diverse others, and seeing how a multicultural perspective was applicable to their lives remained challenging throughout the course. Hornak and

Ortiz observed that the strong emotional reaction to critiquing one's past and the overall complexity of the journey toward self-authorship and a multicultural outlook required a true partnership between educator and learner. They concluded, "If diversity educators incorporate the assumptions and principles of the Learning Partnerships Model in their multicultural educational efforts, students would be more likely to see themselves as intimately involved in culture as it is perpetuated and culture as it is changed" (pp. 121–122).

Although the multicultural education framework is particularly helpful for White students, Ortiz and Rhoads (2000) advocate its utility for students of color as well. Because the model involves exploring aspects of one's own culture and its influence, students can deepen their racial self-understanding through these steps.

Intergroup Dialogue. The University of Michigan's intergroup dialogue approach brings two or more social identity groups together in conversation to promote understanding of social identity issues and facilitate the formation of productive relationships across differences to work toward equity and social justice (Schoem and Hurtado, 2001; Zúñiga, 2003). Like the multicultural education framework, the intergroup dialogue four-stage approach acknowledges students' varied development with a cumulative curriculum. Recognizing students' discomfort with dialogue across differences, stage one focuses on developing an atmosphere conducive to meaningful conversation. Students learn about each other, share insights about their own social identities, establish expectations for dialogue, and learn dialogic skills. This situates learning in their experiences, validates their abilities to participate in shaping the dialogue, and sets the tone for the mutual construction of meaning.

The complexity of knowledge construction and role of the self in that process emerges clearly in stage two, in which students share their social identity experience and situate it within larger social systems. An increased emphasis on talking and listening to each other provides the support needed for the initiation of dialogues regarding the inequitable distribution of privilege. Meeting within homogeneous social identity groups prior to engagement in mixed identity groups is one way of validating students' perspectives to develop their readiness for exploring potentially contrasting perspectives. Exploring controversies and conflict that might arise during discussion reveals the complexity and social construction of knowledge, as well as how the self is integral to establishing particular perspectives. Intergroup dialogue facilitators continue to validate students as knowers during these dialogues and encourage the mutual construction of meaning.

The final stage moves to action planning and alliance building. Students explore how they can use their insights from the intergroup dialogue in future efforts to promote equity. This last stage encourages participants to share authority and expertise in shaping the campus and larger social environments.

Three pedagogical processes permeate all four stages. Sustained communication is requisite for helping students understand conflicting needs and perspectives. Learning dialogic techniques at the outset situates learning in students' experiences and enables them to join an engaging conversation. Critical social awareness is central to helping students question and analyze beliefs, behaviors, and social systems that contribute to tensions among groups. This pedagogical process reveals knowledge as complex and socially constructed and emphasizes the role of self in constructing social identity perspectives. Bridge building, a third process, "begins to build bridges across differences when students can engage in difficult conversations, find value in each other's feelings or perspectives, establish areas of common concern, and be willing to work—separately or together—to counter some of the effects of social injustice" (Zúñiga, 2003, p. 11).

Summarizing earlier findings of Hurtado (2001) and Stephan and Stephan (2001), Zúñiga reported a list of positive outcomes, including increased understanding of social groups, discrimination, stereotypes, and prejudice; improved self-awareness; development of complex thinking; reduced anxiety about interacting with diverse others; enhanced skill in interacting with diverse others; and a greater likelihood of engagement in social justice work. These outcomes reinforce the notion that the balance of challenge and support inherent in the LPM and intergroup dialogue enables growth toward intercultural maturity. Parker (2006) describes a similar process, sustained dialogue, that also moves from relationship building to collective action intended to transform individuals and campus communities to improve racial climates.

Listening Partners. The Listening Partners Project was designed to "promote the development of voice and mind so as to enable women to name, question, and overcome the stereotypes that had left them feeling so diminished" (Belenky, Bond, and Weinstock, 1997, p. 69). The participants were poor, rural mothers, ages seventeen to thirty-four, of preschool-aged children, and their social identities were characterized by socioeconomic disadvantage and geographical isolation rather than race. The approach of the project, which promotes self-authorship and intercultural maturity and is based on *Women's Ways of Knowing* (Belenky, Clinchy, Goldberger, and Tarule, 1986), offered a developmental curriculum that reflected the kind of challenges and support found in the LPM.

Dialogue played a key role for the women regardless of their ways of making meaning on entrance into the project. A major goal was to enable participants to be heard by others and to listen to themselves. Thus, creating safe conversation space was essential because most participants did not value their own voices. Facilitators recorded conversations on newsprint and provided typed copies to participants for further reflection. This effort validated participants as knowers with worthwhile contributions and situated learning in their experiences. Similarly, in meetings, the women were offered prompts such as "I spoke up when . . ." to help publicly reflect on their thinking. Having the participants interview each other and draw out each woman's life story of her aspirations and realizations, which facilitators then typed, copied, and distributed to participants and sometimes to others outside the group, emphasized self as central to knowledge construction and validated each woman's voice. Participants helped each other develop these stories in a mutual construction of knowledge.

Finally, a focus on problem solving encompassed all six components of the LPM. A problem-solving worksheet contained questions to help participants frame problems about which they were concerned, gather ideas from the listening partners about possible solutions, identify the most promising solutions and explore their consequences, and begin to try out alternative resolutions to these complex problems. This activity situated learning in participants' experiences, validated them as knowers, emphasized self as central to solving the problems, revealed the complexity and social construction of the problems posed, and modeled sharing of authority and expertise in sorting through the problems and potential solutions. Participants were encouraged to use the worksheets at home with their families to address everyday challenges with partners or children in thoughtful ways.

Coordinators of the project assessed its effects by interviewing participants before, immediately on completion of the eight-month program, and again nine months later. A control group of nonparticipants, matched for relevant characteristics, served as a base of comparison for growth. Participants in the project reported taking more control over their lives than they had at the outset of the project and reaching out more to acquire needed support from community resources than did nonparticipants. Participants reported a new ability to "think more about others and simultaneously stand up for [themselves]" (Belenky, Bond, and Weinstock, 1997, p. 119), indicating growth in voice, mind, and action. Respondents' dialogue skills increased, and they were better able to participate in mutually growth-enhancing relationships in their families. They left the project with an enhanced appreciation of themselves as capable people and a greater ability to connect with others, as evidenced in participation in community organizations to improve the lives of women and children. This project demonstrates that the challenges and supports of the LPM are productive in contexts where marginalized individuals have minimal support, such as college and university campuses.

Applying the Learning Partnerships Model

We return now to the informal dialogue series with the student organization representatives described at the beginning of this chapter to explore how the LPM can help the six participants engage in a productive dialogue about racial awareness and differences and simultaneously promote their intercultural maturity. The small group crosses the initial, intermediate, and mature ranges of development. Although the facilitator offered an open invitation and refrained from judging their comments, which yielded a lively discussion, it is apparent that some of the students did not actively listen to each other. At the outset of the next meeting, the dean of students could engage the group in getting to know each other and establishing collectively the expectations for their dialogue, an important phase of the intergroup dialogue approach. Because some had already shared initial insights about their own racial experiences, getting to know each other would also assist group members in learning about someone else's racial perspectives. This concurrently validates students' abilities to construct their own perspectives and challenges them to consider that others construct their ideas differently based on their experiences.

The dean's intention to gauge students' perspectives on the campus climate offers an opportunity to situate learning in their experiences. He could assist them in developing a plan to access their peers' viewpoints, thus sharing authority and expertise. This plan could include soliciting feedback on the climate from their respective organizations, conducting focus groups, and observing everyday activities on campus with the goal of crafting implications for the campus climate. These efforts would situate learning directly in students' experiences and help them understand that culture and people mutually shape each other. The organization representatives should be asked to bring these data back to their informal dialogues with the dean and work collaboratively to analyze the campus climate. These dialogues would challenge students to bring themselves to the process of interpreting the data and constructing their perspectives, challenge them to work mutually and interdependently, and convey knowledge as complex and socially constructed.

In addition to refraining from judging students' comments, as the dean did so well in the opening dialogue, he would need to draw out differences of opinion and ask students to explore why they might be coming at an issue differently. Engaging the students in reflecting on how they developed their perspectives would help them process the effects of their own racial histories on current viewpoints. This would be particularly crucial for Doug and Rachel in deconstructing their White identities and would help the other students further their racial identity development as well. These reflections make self central to knowledge construction, validate learners as knowers, and situate learning in their experiences.

Often educators find it difficult to work with a group in which stark developmental differences among students exist. In this instance, as is most often the case, the dean can take advantage of Kendra's maturity and Jonah's and Lester's intermediate development to create partnerships among the student representatives. Kendra's ideas will aid Jonah and Lester in envisioning a mature identity; their intermediate perspectives will offer hope for Rachel's exploration. And Rachel's openness may be helpful to Doug and Valerie in reflecting on their respective racial identities. Validating all of them as capable of constructing a perspective, engaging them in direct experiences that help them learn about the concept of culture and how it affects them personally, and involving them in mutual, interdependent work with each other can help a racially diverse group of students participate in this challenging discussion and grow personally from it. The dialogues also provide the dean with insights into how to engage the larger student body in similar work to move toward self-authorship and intercultural maturity, thereby improving the campus racial climate.

References

Baxter Magolda, M. B. *Making Their Own Way: Narratives for Transforming Higher Education to Promote Self-Development*. Sterling, Va.: Stylus, 2001.

Baxter Magolda, M. B. "Learning Partnerships Model: A Framework for Promoting Self-Authorship." In M. B. Baxter Magolda and P. M. King (eds.), *Learning Partnerships: Theory and Models of Practice to Educate for Self-Authorship*. Sterling, Va.: Stylus, 2004.

Belenky, M. F., Bond, L. A., and Weinstock, J. S. *A Tradition That Has No Name: Nurturing the Development of People, Families, and Communities*. New York: Basic Books, 1997.

Belenky, M., Clinchy, B. M., Goldberger, N., and Tarule, J. *Women's Ways of Knowing: The Development of Self, Voice, and Mind*. New York: Basic Books, 1986.

Hornak, A., and Ortiz, A. M. "Creating a Context to Promote Diversity Education and Self-Authorship Among Community College Students." In M. B. Baxter Magolda and P. M. King (eds.), *Learning Partnerships: Theory and Models of Practice to Educate for Self-Authorship*. Sterling, Va.: Stylus, 2004.

Hurtado, S. "Research and Evaluation on Intergroup Dialogues." In D. Schoem and S. Hurtado (eds.), *Intergroup Dialogue: Deliberative Democracy in School, College, Community, and Workplace*. Ann Arbor: University of Michigan Press, 2001.

Kegan, R. *In over Our Heads: The Mental Demands of Modern Life*. Cambridge, Mass.: Harvard University Press, 1994.

King, P. M., and Baxter Magolda, M. B. "A Developmental Model of Intercultural Maturity." *Journal of College Student Development*, 2005, 46(6), 571–592.

Ortiz, A. M., and Rhoads, R. A. "Deconstructing Whiteness as Part of a Multicultural Educational Framework: From Theory to Practice." *Journal of College Student Development*, 2000, 41(1), 81–93.

Parker, P. "Sustained Dialogue: How Students Are Changing Their Own Racial Climate." *About Campus*, 2006, 11(1), 17–23.

Schoem, D., and Hurtado, S. *Intergroup Dialogue: Deliberative Democracy in School, College, Community, and Workplace*. Ann Arbor: University of Michigan Press, 2001.

Stephan, W., and Stephan, C. *Improving Intergroup Relations*. Thousand Oaks, Calif.: Sage, 2001.

Zúñiga, X. "Bridging Differences Through Dialogue." *About Campus*, 2003, 7(6), 8–16.

STEPHEN JOHN QUAYE *is assistant professor in the College Student Personnel Program at the University of Maryland, College Park.*

MARCIA B. BAXTER MAGOLDA *is Distinguished Professor of Educational Leadership at Miami University.*

NEW DIRECTIONS FOR STUDENT SERVICES • DOI: 10.1002/ss

This chapter examines color-blind campuses that perpetu-
ate White transparency and racially cognizant environ-
ments that reveal and challenge notions of color
blindness. Recommendations are offered to help White
students respond to the realities of Whiteness and move
beyond color-blind racism.

5

The Complicated Realities of Whiteness: From Color Blind to Racially Cognizant

Robert D. Reason, Nancy J. Evans

Some authors have argued that White transparency—the belief that Whites can move through life without examining their own racial identities—is a thing of the past (Giroux, 1997). The increasingly diverse nature of college campuses, along with required diversity courses and the prevalence of racial sensitivity workshops, appear to make this belief especially true for White students on college campuses. Implied in this perspective is the assumption that White students can proceed through the college experience without having fully examined their race. We disagree.

The very nature of academic environments continues to perpetuate multiple characteristics that excuse White students from seriously taking the time to examine the role of race (their own and others) in their lives. Several authors (Tatum, 1997; Willie, 2003) have described the pervasiveness of Whiteness on college campuses due to the visible racially dominant population, traditions, and culture that cater to White people, whereas others have simply labeled higher education a "White space" (Feagin, Vera, and Imani, 1996; Kivel, 2004; Purwar, 2004) because of the invisible control exerted by the culture of Whiteness on campuses. Unfortunately, as Frankenberg (1993) pointed out, "Whiteness, as a set of normative cultural practices, is visible most clearly to those it definitively excludes and those to whom it does violence. Those who are securely housed within its borders usually do not examine it" (p. 228), nor are they challenged to do so.

NEW DIRECTIONS FOR STUDENT SERVICES, no. 120, Winter 2007   © Wiley Periodicals, Inc.
Published online in Wiley InterScience (www.interscience.wiley.com) • DOI: 10.1002/ss.258

This chapter examines the types of college environments that perpetuate White transparency and those environments that challenge it. Although our focus is on environments, we do not lose sight of the White students who operate within them. Students both act on and are acted on by the environments in which they live. The realities of race for White students on college campuses are complicated, manifold, and often difficult. For some White students, race does not matter; Whiteness is not a salient feature of their identities and remains unexamined. These students subscribe to a color-blind ideology. For other White students, race assumes a high level of saliency, resulting in a nuanced self-understanding and greater propensity toward racial justice actions (Reason, Roosa Millar, and Scales, 2005). Although these are two ends of the continuum, and most White students likely fall somewhere between these two poles, we propose that creating environments that move White students toward greater racial saliency will result in better outcomes for all students.

In the next section, we examine the nature of color-blind environments and highlight the attitudes and actions of people in these environments that perpetuate color-blind racism. We then focus on racially cognizant environments and the importance such environments have in helping students move beyond color-blind ideologies toward greater self-awareness and awareness of others. We close by offering recommendations and actions to consider in responding to the realities of Whiteness.

Color-Blind Environments

Forman (2004) argued that the racial ideology that developed after the civil rights era in the United States is best described as color-blind racism. He explained that many Americans assert that they no longer view race as important or state that they "do not see race" (p. 45). Moreover, polls suggest that racism is viewed as something that this country has overcome as a result of civil rights legislation and that Americans believe that people of color are doing as well as Whites (Gallagher, 2003). Any current inequalities among racial or ethnic groups are seen as resulting from nonracial factors, such as class differences or personal attributes and choices (Forman, 2004).

Forman (2004) identified four beliefs associated with color-blind racism: (1) racial groups receive privileges based on merit, (2) most people do not care about or pay attention to race, (3) patterns of social inequity are the result of cultural deficits of individuals or racial/ethnic groups, and (4) because of these three factors, no systematic attention needs to be given to any existing inequities.

The belief that racism is a thing of the past is grounded in the individualistic perspective on racism held by most Americans (Scheurich and Young, 2002). Racism, as typically defined, involves overt actions of an aggressive or blatantly discriminatory nature taken by one person against another because of that person's race. As Rains (1998) noted, "Undergirding this construction is a logic that alleges individuals who are not engaged in overtly racist behaviors are not racist" (p. 81). And, by extension, if one does not engage in racist acts, one does not have to think about them. As a result of this belief system, the true structural, institutional, and societal causes of inequity go unnoticed, and efforts to address these causes are viewed as illegitimate and unnecessary (Forman, 2004).

At the same time, individuals who are members of the dominant group deny feelings of prejudice against other racial/ethnic groups and find socially acceptable ways to express disapproval, for example, by defending traditional values, exaggerating cultural differences, or focusing on personality traits (Forman, 2004). Racial apathy, defined as indifference to inequality and lack of action in the face of racial injustice, is another method through which color-blind racism is expressed. Forman reported that 21 percent of White youth surveyed in 2000 indicated that race relations in the United States do not concern them.

Color-blind racism can be partially attributed to lack of knowledge (Forman, 2004). Many Americans are unaware of the discrimination that exists in society because they have no direct contact with it. Americans live in an increasingly segregated society, and Whites are the most segregated racial group in the country (Forman, 2004). This finding applies to housing and education (Lewis and others, 2004). Many, if not most, White children attend schools with few students from other racial and ethnic groups, a situation that is growing worse. Examining national data, Frankenberg and Lee (2002) found that "virtually all school districts analyzed are showing lower levels of inter-racial exposure since 1986" (p. 4). Thus, students enter college with little exposure to and little concern for the issues facing members of other racial groups.

While racial and ethnic diversity, as well as support services for students of color, have increased on many college campuses, an extensive review of research indicated that increased White consciousness has not resulted (Hurtado, Milem, Clayton-Pederson, and Allen, 1998). Color-blind racism takes many subtle forms in college settings, including attitudes and behaviors exhibited by White students, faculty, and staff; the assumptions underlying the services provided for students; and the policy decisions that affect student recruitment and enrollment. A few examples follow.

College students often express the attitudes that Forman (2004) associated with color-blind racism in a number of ways. For example, consider the results from a study (Ellis, 2004) conducted with 150 White students attending a community college in the Los Angeles area, the most ethnically diverse city in the United States, where 77 percent of the enrolled students were people of color. Respondents reported that race/ethnicity was not an issue for them and that too much importance was placed on racial/ethnic differences. In addition, half of the respondents obtained low scores on a measure of ethnic identity, indicating that they were largely unaware of racial/ethnic differences.

The actions of students also reflect their color-blind attitudes. Very few students in Ellis's study (2004) had not taken multicultural or ethnic studies courses, and they had not dealt with experiences that led them to question their attitudes. Even students participating in a multicultural leadership program at a midwestern research institution indicated that they had little contact with individuals of other races in their home communities or on campus; twenty-nine of the forty-four students had taken minimal or no course work examining multicultural issues, and twenty-three had attended one or no program focusing on a multicultural topic (Evans and others, 2005). Changes in attitudes require social interaction and involvement at a level beyond casual contact (Hurtado, Milem, Clayton-Pedersen, and Allen, 1998). But a survey of students from 390 colleges revealed that when compared to Chicano, Asian American, and African American students, White students were least likely to engage in activities (such as sharing meals, rooming, socializing, or dating) with individuals of other races (Hurtado, Dey, and Treviño as cited in Hurtado, Milem, Clayton-Pedersen, and Allen, 1998).

Stage and Manning (1992) pointed out six assumptions underlying the manner in which colleges and universities work with students; these assumptions appear to be based on color-blind racist attitudes and are still guiding practice today. First, students of color are expected to adjust to the college environment, which is almost always White and Eurocentric in structure. For instance, university calendars provide no latitude for American Indian students to attend religious ceremonies or other cultural events on their reservations. Second, the expectation is that non-White faculty, staff, or students will be responsible for any initiative to address non-White cultural issues. For example, when diversity training is done, it is usually assumed that people of color will do it. Third, students of color are assumed to have interests that are similar to those of White students. When they wish to join race-specific organizations or fail to become involved in "color-blind" organizations such as student government or the student programming board, they are criticized. Fourth, and conversely, when students of color fail to take part in academic support programs provided for them by the university, they are viewed as ungrateful and lazy. Assuming that all students of color need academic support is a critical mistake that sends a negative message to high-achieving students. Fifth, an obvious color-blind racist assumption is that all students are provided equitable educational opportunities by colleges and universities. Thus, the environmental challenges that students of color face are ignored. A final overriding assumption is that the dominant White culture through which the university environment functions is working well and requires no adjustment.

NEW DIRECTIONS FOR STUDENT SERVICES • DOI: 10.1002/ss

Racially Cognizant Whiteness

Although most college policies and environments encourage color-blind racism in Whites, some White students manage to move past color blindness to develop a racially cognizant sense of selves. For these students, race becomes a lens through which they can understand daily life on campus and serves as the impetus of their transition toward becoming racially cognizant. The call for such an environment is not new; Ortiz and Rhoads (2000) in their seminal piece on Whiteness posited that an active, advanced understanding of Whiteness was the foundation on which a multicultural outlook was built.

A racially cognizant sense of Whiteness involves a continuous process of rearticulating the meaning of race (Reason, Roosa Millar, and Scales, 2005). What we describe here as a reconstruction others, notably Ortiz and Rhoads (2000), have called a deconstruction of Whiteness. Regardless of the label used, the process involves an active exploration of what it means to be White in American society and likely results in a transition from White as "the color of my skin" to an active reconstructing of a racialized sense of self. A racially cognizant sense of Whiteness encompasses an understanding of guilt, power, and privilege yet avoids the paralysis and victim perspectives that some Whites assume. It involves the translation of this understanding of Whiteness into positive action. Racially cognizant White students tend to exhibit more racial justice attitudes and actions than do color-blind White students. A racially cognizant sense of self seems to be a prerequisite to Whites engaging in the fight for racial justice.

Although the educational benefits of diverse environments are well documented and accepted in higher education (Hurtado, Milem, Clayton-Pedersen, and Allen, 1998), a diverse student body does not guarantee that White students will engage across racial differences or assume a racially cognizant understanding of self. Avoiding critical examinations of Whiteness is relatively easy for White students, even on diverse college campuses (Hu and Kuh, 2003; Reason, Roosa Millar, and Scales, 2005). The development of racially cognizant White students requires student affairs professionals to intentionally create spaces for White students to reflect on the meaning of race in their daily lives.

Findings from Perry's ethnographic study (2002) of two distinct California high schools—one predominantly White, the other racially and ethnically heterogeneous—reinforce the importance of an engaging peer culture coupled with structural diversity in formulating a racially cognizant sense of Whiteness. Although completed in secondary education settings, Perry's research is supported by, and supports, findings from similar studies in postsecondary settings (see, for example, Reason, Roosa Millar, and Scales, 2005, and Roosa Millar, 2006).

The racial composition of the two environments provided very different experiences regarding race for the White students at each school, which resulted in different understandings of Whiteness. For students in the racially homogeneous high school, Whiteness was understood as "normal" (Perry, 2002, p. 181). These students were not challenged to explore race in any meaningful manner and held a shallow understanding of their own racial identities. Ortiz and Rhoads (2000) suggested that students who accept Whiteness as normal fail to develop any meaningful racial consciousness and are more likely to resist efforts to develop a deeper understanding.

The White students in Perry's study (2002) who experienced a racially heterogeneous environment demonstrated a much more reflective understanding of race and Whiteness. These students constructed a discursive, problematic racial understanding. Their experiences in the school environment made race much more salient, and often more contentious, which forced students of all races to confront and work through racialized situations. The White students demonstrated a more thoughtful understanding of Whiteness, a more nuanced sense of Whites as multicultural beings, and greater skills at interacting across racial and ethnic differences. Perry observed that deep, meaningful interactions across racial differences were part of the culture of this school and essential to the development of students' sense of Whiteness.

Findings from research related to racial justice allies (Neville Miller and Harris, 2005; Reason, Roosa Millar, and Scales, 2005) reveal the importance of course work related to race, White role models, and invitations allowing White students to engage in the critical examination of race. Specific courses and programs that focus on "the multiple meanings of whiteness and their effects on the way white consciousness is historically structured and socially inscribed" (Kincheloe, 1999, p. 163) are necessary to provide White students the cognitive understanding to explore Whiteness. These multiple meanings of Whiteness must incorporate knowledge of power and privilege, including the privileges associated with choosing a color-blind perspective. Such courses and programs must create spaces for White students to thoughtfully and safely engage with and challenge preconceived, and unexamined, notions of Whiteness (Roosa Millar, 2006).

To move from the familiarity of color-blind racism toward a racially cognizant understanding, White students need guidance and opportunity (Reason, Roosa Millar, and Scales, 2005). They need White role models who demonstrate a commitment to critically examining Whiteness and the propensity to actively reject color-blind racism, even when such rejection may harm their self-interest. White role models often also provide the invitation for White students to test their new understandings of Whiteness through racial justice actions (Broido, 2000; Reason, Roosa Millar, and Scales, 2005).

Although racialized environments likely produce many positive outcomes for White students, they can be both foreign and painful for White students (Bishop, 2002). This acknowledgment is not meant to apologize or create excuses for Whites; rather, it reminds us that White students need support during this process. When White students examine their own sense of Whiteness and acknowledge the accompanying privilege (and the racism on which that privilege is built and maintained), painful emotions likely follow. As Thompson (2003) concluded, "When old values prove false, the loss we feel in giving up the sense of selfhood tied to those values is painful" (p. 21). Racially cognizant Whites must accept that the privilege of ignoring race (color blindness) has been replaced by the pain of acknowledging that race and racism are part of their identities (Thompson, 2003).

Responding to the Realities of Whiteness

This chapter has presented two realities of Whiteness. First, the color-blind reality is deeply rooted in the belief that "good" White people can and comfortably do ignore race. This view is also grounded in the hegemony of individuality—any existing inequalities are a result of personal problems rather than racism—a worldview that maintains a particularly pernicious form of racism. Many current policies in higher education perpetuate color-blind racism, which is ultimately displayed in students' actions and their attitudes toward others. White students who move past a color-blind worldview move toward the second reality of Whiteness we explored in this chapter: a racially cognizant sense of Whiteness. This sense of Whiteness is characterized by the continuous and perpetual examination of the role of race in our lives, involves openness to the painful emotions that accompany the realization that privilege and racism are part of our racial identities, and seems to be associated with a greater propensity toward racial justice actions.

If we hope to move White students toward a more racially cognizant Whiteness, we as educators must create spaces in which White students can "narrate their own racialized history, identify themselves as white, catalog the unearned advantages they accrue because they are white, and demonstrate their willingness to claim themselves as racist. . . . However, to remain antiracism activists they must find a way to balance this negative identity with some positive constructions of self—or they will not be able to continue the work" (Eichstedt, 2001, p. 465). We do so by breaking the cycle that reproduces color-blind racism and by moving our students toward a more racially cognizant sense of Whiteness.

White students must learn to balance the desire to view each person as an individual, with recognition of the role that social group membership plays in shaping an individual's experiences. Importantly, one of the most difficult realities for White students to grasp might be the role that social group membership plays in their own lives. Recognizing that Whiteness is a social identity is particularly difficult for students who have been taught to think of racial and ethnic identity as applying only to individuals of color and to ignore the role that race and ethnicity play in their own overall life experience. To overcome such attitudes, it is particularly important to encourage courses and programs specifically related to the exploration of Whiteness, power, and privilege. Recent research demonstrates the powerful educational benefits of a focus on Whiteness, arguing for exposing students to a focused study of Whiteness rather than simply adding Whiteness to other "diversity courses."

NEW DIRECTIONS FOR STUDENT SERVICES • DOI: 10.1002/ss

Moving students toward a racially cognizant sense of Whiteness also requires that we who claim a White identity discuss with our students what it means to be White and also encourage students to reflect on their Whiteness. In so doing, we should be intentionally disrupting the unexamined hegemony of Whiteness that allows students to honestly, yet erroneously, believe that race does not matter.

References

Bishop, A. *Becoming an Ally: Breaking the Cycle of Oppression in People.* (2nd ed.) Halifax, Nova Scotia: Fernwood, 2002.

Broido, E. M. "The Development of Social Justice Allies During College: A Phenomenological Investigation." *Journal of College Student Development,* 2000, *41,* 3–18.

Eichstedt, J. L. "Problematic White Identities and a Search for Racial Justice." *Sociological Forum,* 2001, *16,* 445–470.

Ellis, P. H. "White Identity Development at a Two-Year Institution." *Community College Journal of Research and Practice,* 2004, *28,* 745–761.

Evans, N. J., Olsen, S., Conroy, M., Pederson, M., and Helling, J. "Multicultural Leadership Summit 2005: Final Evaluation Report." Unpublished document, Iowa State University, 2005.

Feagin, J. R., Vera, H., and Imani, N. *The Agony of Education: Black Students at White Colleges and Universities.* New York: Routledge, 1996.

Forman, T. A. "Color-Blind Racism and Racial Indifference: The Role of Racial Apathy in Facilitating Enduring Inequalities." In M. Krysan and A. E. Lewis (eds.), *The Changing Terrain of Race and Ethnicity.* New York: Russell Sage Foundation, 2004.

Frankenberg, E., and Lee, C. *Race in American Public Schools: Rapidly Resegregating School Districts.* Cambridge, Mass.: Harvard University, Harvard Civil Rights Project, 2002.

Frankenberg, R. *The Social Construction of Whiteness: White Women, Race Matters.* Minneapolis: University of Minnesota Press, 1993.

Gallagher, C. A. "Color-Blind Privilege: The Social and Political Functions of Erasing the Color Line in Post Race America." *Race, Class, and Gender,* 2003, *10*(4), 22–37.

Giroux, H. A. "Rewriting the Discourse of Racial Identity: Towards a Pedagogy and Politics of Whiteness." *Harvard Educational Review,* 1997, *67*(2), 285–320.

Hu, S., and Kuh, G. D. "Diversity Experiences and College Student Learning and Personal Development." *Journal of College Student Development,* 2003, *44,* 320–334.

Hurtado, S., Milem, J. F., Clayton-Pedersen, A., and Allen, W. R. "Enhancing Campus Climates for Racial/Ethnic Diversity: Educational Policy and Practice." *Review of Higher Education,* 1998, *21*(3), 279–302.

Kincheloe, J. L. "The Struggle to Define and Reinvent Whiteness: A Pedagogical Analysis." *College Literature,* 1999, *26,* 162–194.

Kivel, P. "The Culture of Power." In F. W. Hale Jr. (ed.), *What Makes Racial Diversity Work in Higher Education: Academic Leaders Present Successful Policies and Strategies.* Sterling, Va.: Stylus, 2004.

Lewis, A. E., and others. "Institutional Patterns and Transformations: Race and Ethnicity in Housing, Education, Labor Markets, Religion, and Criminal Justice." In M. Krysan and A. E. Lewis (eds.), *The Changing Terrain of Race and Ethnicity.* New York: Russell Sage Foundation, 2004.

Neville Miller, A., and Harris, T. M. "Communicating to Develop White Racial Identity in an Interracial Communication Class." *Communication Education,* 2005, *54,* 223–242.

Ortiz, A. M., and Rhoads, R. A. "Deconstructing Whiteness as Part of a Multicultural Educational Framework: From Theory to Practice." *Journal of College Student Development,* 2000, *41,* 81–93.

Perry, P. *Shades of White: White Kids and Racial Identities in High School.* Durham, N.C.: Duke University Press, 2002.

Purwar, N. "Fish in or out of Water: A Theoretical Framework for Race and the Space of Academia." In I. Law, D. Phillips, and L. Turney (eds.), *Institutional Racism in Higher Education.* Sterling, Va.: Trentham, 2004.

Rains, F. V. "Is the Benign Really Harmless? Deconstructing Some 'Benign' Manifestations of Operationalized White Privilege." In J. Kincheloe, S. R. Steinberg, N. M. Rodriguez, and R. E. Chennault (eds.), *White Reign: Deploying Whiteness in America.* New York: St. Martin's Griffin, 1998.

Reason, R. D., Roosa Millar, E. A., and Scales, T. C. "Toward a Model of Racial Justice Ally Development in College." *Journal of College Student Development,* 2005, *46,* 530–546.

Roosa Millar, E. A. "Reflection to Action: A Grounded Case Study of an Intentionally Designed Racial Justice Curriculum." Unpublished doctoral dissertation, The Pennsylvania State University, 2006.

Scheurich, J. J., and Young, M. D. "White Racism Among White Faculty: From Critical Understanding to Antiracist Activism." In W. A. Smith, P. G. Altbach, and K. Lomotey (eds.), *The Racial Crisis in American Higher Education: Continuing Challenges for the Twenty-First Century.* (2nd ed.) Albany: State University of New York Press, 2002.

Stage, F. K., and Manning, K. (eds.). *Enhancing the Multicultural Campus Environment: A Cultural Brokering Approach.* New Directions for Student Services, no. 60. San Francisco: Jossey-Bass, 1992.

Tatum, B. D. *Why Are All the Black Kids Sitting Together in the Cafeteria? And Other Conversations About Race.* New York: Basic Books, 1997.

Thompson, A. "Tiffany, Friend of People of Color: White Investments in Antiracism." *Qualitative Studies in Education,* 2003, *16*(1), 7–29.

Willie, S. S. *Acting Black: College, Identity, and the Performance of Race.* New York: Routledge, 2003.

ROBERT D. REASON *is assistant professor and research associate in the Center for the Study of Higher Education at The Pennsylvania State University.*

NANCY J. EVANS *is professor of higher education in the Department of Educational Leadership and Policy Studies at Iowa State University.*

NEW DIRECTIONS FOR STUDENT SERVICES • DOI: 10.1002/ss

6

The Equity Scorecard, a nationally recognized and widely used organizational learning process designed to foster institutional change through the identification and elimination of racial disparities among college students, is described in this chapter. The effectiveness of this process and its potential impact are also discussed.

The Equity Scorecard: A Collaborative Approach to Assess and Respond to Racial/Ethnic Disparities in Student Outcomes

Frank Harris III, Estela Mara Bensimon

Despite recent efforts to increase accountability in higher education, racial/ethnic disparities in student outcomes are a reality at most of the nation's colleges and universities (Bensimon, 2004). Disparate completion rates and a host of inequitable outcomes between racial/ethnic minorities and White students persist. Although most states have accountability systems, equity has not been incorporated as an indicator of institutional accountability or as an aspirational benchmark. Moreover, while many institutions monitor minute changes in the average SAT scores of entering first-year students obsessively, they do not keep track of how effectively they are performing based on the production of successful outcomes for minority students (Bensimon, Hao, and Bustillos, 2006). Neither external accountability systems nor internal institutional reports incorporate measures that would enable policymakers or institutional leaders to answer questions such as, "What proportion of African American students who earned bachelor degrees in 2007 had a cumulative grade point average of 3.5 or higher?" or "What proportion of a community college's Latina/o students are in the honors program that guarantees transfer to selective four-year colleges?"

Also, little attention is paid to how institutions can be more proactive in increasing the number of African American and Latina/o students who

New Directions for Student Services, no. 120, Winter 2007 © Wiley Periodicals, Inc.
Published online in Wiley InterScience (www.interscience.wiley.com) • DOI: 10.1002/ss.259

graduate from college with high grade point averages (Gándara, 1999). By all indications, what institutions seem to pay attention to is whether they are admitting sufficient numbers of minority students and whether, once admitted, those students survive academically. The need for intentional monitoring of minority students' educational outcomes is made clear by Massey, Charles, Lundy, and Fisher (2003), whose analysis led them to conclude that "despite a variety of retention efforts . . . once admitted to institutions of higher education, African Americans and Latinos/as continually underperform relative to their White and Asian counterparts, earning lower grades, progressing at a slower pace, and dropping out at higher rates" (p. 2).

We assert that leaders in higher education pay attention to what is measured (Bensimon, 2004; Birnbaum, 1988), so it follows that if the academic outcomes of minority students are not assessed regularly and treated as measurable evidence of institutional performance, we can expect inequalities in outcomes to remain structurally hidden and unattended to. We believe that collecting data on student outcomes disaggregated by race and reporting on them regularly should be a standard operating practice in colleges and universities. At the same time, we also recognize that the value of student outcome data depends on the capacity and willpower of institutions to transform data into actionable knowledge. As Dowd (2005) points out, data provide information but in and of themselves do not drive change. People make change happen. Data are necessary for organizational learning (Argyris and Schön, 1996), but without people who have the willingness to become engaged with the data and have the know-how to unpack data tables by asking questions, looking for patterns, forming hunches, challenging interpretations, and putting a story to those data, the knowledge contained in data will be concealed and unavailable. Indeed, most accountability systems, in both K–12 and in higher education, lack the structures, tools, and processes to be an effective means of organizational learning. Postsecondary institutions are rich in data but poor in the means and know-how of organizational learning. The barriers to organizational learning inherent in the structure and culture of institutions of higher education are explanatory factors for the limited impact accountability systems have within the classroom, the counseling center, the student activities office, and the learning resources center, among others.

Recognizing that data and campus-level practitioners are at the heart of organizational learning and change, researchers at the University of Southern California's Center for Urban Education created an intervention that involves practitioners in data practices designed to create new knowledge and bring about change within themselves and their institutions (Bauman, 2005; Bauman and others, 2005; Bensimon, 2004; Bensimon, Polkinghorne, Bauman, and Vallejo, 2004; Pena, Bensimon, and Colyar, 2006). This intervention, which goes by the name of Equity Scorecard, is being implemented in two- and four-year public and independent colleges throughout California, the University of Wisconsin system, and several

NEW DIRECTIONS FOR STUDENT SERVICES • DOI: 10.1002/ss

other states. In this chapter, we describe the principles of the Equity Score-card as well as its core components.

The Equity Scorecard: A Learning and Change Intervention

Modeled after the Balanced Scorecard for business (see Kaplan and Norton, 1992) and the Academic Scorecard for Higher Education (see O'Neil, Bensimon, Diamond, and Moore, 1999), the idea for the Equity Scorecard was initially developed when it became evident that equity, although valued, is not measured in relation to educational outcomes for traditionally marginalized students in higher education. The scorecard is a tool and an established process to develop evidence-based awareness of race-based inequities among practitioners and to instill a sense of responsibility for addressing these gaps. Simply put, the outcome sought through the Equity Scorecard is for campus practitioners, including presidents, faculty members, counselors, deans, and directors, to become local experts on the educational outcomes of minority students within their own campus and to come to view these outcomes as a matter of institutional responsibility.

These two goals (awareness of outcomes inequities and accountability for eradicating inequitable outcomes) are stressed for two reasons. First, we have found that campus participants in institutions that are racially diverse, in fact even in minority-serving institutions (Contreras, Malcom, and Bensimon, forthcoming), are often impervious to racially stratified educational outcomes. Second, when race-based disparities become evident, campus actors are more likely to externalize the problem and attribute it to student characteristics or circumstances that lessen their own responsibility or institutional fault (Bensimon, 2007). The prevalence of special compensatory programs to address the educational and social needs of minority students on virtually every college campus is indicative of the extent to which student success is understood as being primarily a student responsibility. Although we do not deny the power of individual student agency to determine the quality of the collegiate experience, we also believe that institutions have a responsibility for creating the necessary conditions for equitable educational outcomes. Just as institutions are now expected to be accountable for student retention and graduation, the same expectation should be held for equity. Institutions, through their policies as well as the practices, attitudes, and knowledge of their members, have the power to create the conditions that make student success possible or perpetuate race-based inequalities.

Unlike the great majority of campus interventions intended for minority students, the Equity Scorecard is an intervention designed to create learning and change among practitioners. The prevalence of inequality, we believe, reflects a learning problem of practitioners. Specifically, the taken-for-granted knowledge that practitioners have acquired over time about

NEW DIRECTIONS FOR STUDENT SERVICES • DOI: 10.1002/ss

teaching and learning, and which they have found to be effective in the past, now may be failing them. Many faculty members lament that students today are not like the students from the past. This jeremiad is often heard on campuses that, as a consequence of unplanned demographic changes, are experiencing a cultural chasm between their predominantly White faculty and predominantly minority students.

Higher education practitioners have been socialized to a model of teaching and learning that is based on individualism; thus, when students do not do well academically, we are inclined to look into their behaviors for explanations. For example, we may notice that the student has not attempted to seek assistance during designated office hours or take advantage of the tutoring services that are available in the learning center. Lack of cultural knowledge may keep us from noticing the ways in which we, unknowingly and unintendedly, create the conditions that prevent students from behaving according to our expectations (Pena, Bensimon, and Colyar, 2006; Steele, 1997).

Simply stated, the learning problem of institutions and practitioners lies in the failure to recognize that one's best practices may not be effective with students who are not familiar with the hidden curriculum of how to be a successful college student. The challenge is to uncover what might enable educational practitioners to address unequal educational outcomes among minority students as a problem of institutional and practitioner knowledge.

The Equity Scorecard as a Means of Learning and Change

The guiding principle of the Equity Scorecard is that "learning and change are made possible by the engagement of practitioners in a collaborative and productive activity setting" (Bensimon, Polkinghorne, Bauman, and Vallejo, 2004; Wenger, 1998). By practitioners, we mean just about any campus professional whose beliefs, knowledge, and practices can affect the outcomes of minority students. For example, extremely high percentages of new minority students are placed in noncredit basic math and English courses. One of the biggest obstacles to minority student success is getting through basic math courses successfully, and a great number of students drop out without ever having taken a college-level math course. In the Equity Scorecard framework, the basic skills math instructors are practitioners whose unconscious actions, informed by tacit knowledge, can be a tremendous source of motivation and support for minority students—or one of despair and self-doubt.

Accordingly, the involvement of math instructors as members of an Equity Scorecard team is a means of increasing their awareness with the hope of moving them to reflect on the role they can play to ameliorate unequal outcomes. The same is true for counselors who help students plan their future, administrators who control the allocation of resources, program directors who oversee student support services, and so on (for a more in-depth discussion of the theoretical grounding of these ideas, see Bensimon,

Polkinghorne, Bauman, and Vallejo, 2004; Bensimon, 2007; Pena, Bensimon, and Colyar, 2006).

The means of engaging practitioners in a collaborative activity is by the formation of small campus teams that typically work together for a year, meeting monthly for about two hours. The activity on which these teams collaborate involves making sense of easily accessible institutional data that are disaggregated by race and ethnicity. During the meetings, team members collaborate by examining the disaggregated data collectively, raising questions about the data, deciding what additional data they should look at to answer their questions, and challenging others' assumptions and interpretations about the data. In community colleges, one outcome of the teams' collaboration is the creation of an Equity Scorecard with key indicators of student success, organized by four concurrent perspectives: academic pathways, retention and persistence, transfer readiness, and excellence. Each perspective focuses on specific aspects of institutional performance with respect to equity in student outcomes.

Examining Disaggregated Student Outcomes Data. Prior to the first team meeting, we ask the institutional researcher to complete a data spreadsheet that we refer to as the "vital signs." The vital signs consist of data that are routinely collected on most campuses, disaggregated by race/ethnicity. We call them vital signs because they provide insight into the health and status of an institution with respect to equity in student outcomes (Bensimon, Hao, and Bustillos, 2006). For example, "the number and percentage of students who earn an associate degree within six years" is a vital sign for the retention and persistence perspective for the Equity Scorecard. At a community college, "completion of 60 or more transferable units" and "transfer to a four-year institution in three years or less" are vital signs for the transfer readiness and excellence perspectives, respectively. The vital signs provide a starting point for the teams' examination of data by highlighting potential gaps and inequities in student outcomes. The format of the vital signs is tailored for people who are not accustomed to examining data. Based on our observations, the capacity to make sense of data requires specialized practices that are underdeveloped on most college campuses. This is reinforced by a point we made earlier: institutions have a wealth of data but are impoverished in their capacity to make sense of them.

While reviewing and discussing the vital signs data collaboratively, team members are encouraged to ask questions. Say, for instance, that a team discovers a gap among Latino/a students who earn associate degrees. The following questions may be raised by team members: "How many Latino/a students in the cohort indicated that earning the associate degree is their educational goal?" "How many Latino/a students in the cohort have completed the English and math courses that are required for the associate degree?" "How engaged are Latino/a students in educationally purposeful activities that enhance learning and produce desired outcomes?" "Are they earning grades in their courses that would allow them to persist to the completion of the associate degree?" As questions like these are raised about the data, team members discuss and agree on those that should be pursued in subsequent meetings. This step entails deciding what new data they would like the institutional researcher to prepare and present at the next team meeting. For instance, the team may decide to examine data that illustrate students' educational goals in order to learn how many Latino/a students are pursuing an associate degree. The team may also look at student progression through math and English course sequences to see if Latino/a students have completed the associate degree requirement in these subject areas. Finally, to answer questions about students' academic performance, the team may choose to look at grade point averages and course completion rates.

What is unique about this process is that team members take the role of researchers rather than relying on the knowledge produced by outsiders, such as consultants or university researchers. In this research model, the researchers, all team members, assume the role of facilitators and learners. As facilitators, we create the structures, tools, and processes of organizational learning that the great majority of colleges, regardless of selectivity or wealth, lack. As learners, we observe and document the impact of practitioner-driven research as a means of self- and institutional change. That is, we observe whether the math or English instructor, counselor, or others in the team are more open to reconsidering their own practices and how they might change them in order to improve student outcomes.

Constructing an Equity Scorecard. Once the team has gone through the cycle of reviewing vital signs data, discovering potential areas of inequity, asking questions about the data, and reviewing subsequent data, they work collectively to agree on indicators that will be included in the Equity Scorecard they will construct on behalf of the campus. For example, if the team finds that Latino/a students are disproportionately enrolled in basic skills English and math courses that are not applicable to the associate degree, they may decide to include "successful progression from basic skills to college-level English" and "successful progression from basic skills to college-level math" as indicators in the academic pathways perspective of its Equity Scorecard. They may also discover that many Latino/a students do not persist beyond a critical gateway course within the sequence, English 100, for example. Gateway courses are those that serve as entry or exit points to graduation, transfer, or completion of basic skills requirements. Thus, students who are not successful in these courses are disadvantaged in several respects, notably time to degree completion. As such, the team may decide to include "successful completion of English 100" as one of its Equity Scorecard indicators. The team continues this type of analysis and collaborative sense making until they have examined data and developed indicators for all four of the Equity Scorecard perspectives. Once the team has constructed the scorecard, their next task is to disseminate their findings to stakeholders who can use the knowledge to mobilize change.

Sharing Equity Scorecard Findings with Stakeholders. In addition to working collaboratively to learn about the state of equity on behalf of their institution and constructing an Equity Scorecard, team members are charged with disseminating their findings to the campus. As noted in Bensimon, Polkinghorne, Bauman, and Vallejo (2004), "The opportunity for institutional change lies in the possibility that individual participants will transfer their learning to other contexts within the institution, and in doing so, enable others to learn and to change" (p. 113). The teams disseminate their learning and findings by way of a comprehensive written report to the president of the institution. In the report, the team discusses the data that served as the focal points of its analysis, the gaps and inequities they discovered within each perspective, and recommendations for actions and further inquiry. Moreover, throughout the process, the team disseminates its findings by making presentations to stakeholder groups that shape and influence campus policies and practices with a direct impact on equity in student outcomes. The academic senate, strategic planning committee, academic deans, and academic departments in which the most significant inequities exist (for example, math and English) are examples of some of the groups to which the team presents its findings. Finally, team members take their new-found knowledge and awareness of inequities in student outcomes to other committees, task forces, and other groups in which they participate. We ensure that the learning that takes place among the members of the Equity Scorecard team is diffused throughout the campus by including team members who are boundary spanners, serving on institution-wide committees which have access to multiple audiences.

Conclusion

Racial/ethnic disparities in student outcomes are a reality at most colleges and university in the United States. We believe that the intellectual capital and resources that are necessary to respond effectively to this unfortunate reality are often situated within institutions. We also believe that compensatory programs that aim to eliminate racial/ethnic student deficits alone are not sufficient to bring about equity in student outcomes. Alternatively, the Equity Scorecard approach has proven to be an effective institutional learning and change intervention.

Applying Harper and Bensimon's concept of color consciousness (2003), responding to the realities of race requires institutional leaders to focus purposefully and intentionally on equity in student outcomes to ensure that their institutions are welcoming, affirming, and responsive environments for groups that historically have been denied access to the benefits of higher education. The Equity Scorecard provides the means and the context for institutional leaders to develop color-consciousness and thereby build their capacities to assess and respond to race-based disparities in student outcomes.

NEW DIRECTIONS FOR STUDENT SERVICES • DOI: 10.1002/ss

References

Argyris, C., and Schön, D. A. *Organizational Learning II: Theory, Method, and Practice.* Reading, Mass.: Addison-Wesley, 1996.

Bauman, G. L. "Promoting Organizational Learning in Higher Education to Achieve Equity in Educational Outcomes." In A. J. Kezar (ed.), *Organizational Learning in Higher Education.* New Directions for Higher Education, no. 131. San Francisco: Jossey-Bass, 2005.

Bauman, G. L., and others. *Achieving Equitable Educational Outcomes with All Students: The Institution's Roles and Responsibilities.* Washington, D.C.: Association for American Colleges and Universities, 2005.

Bensimon, E. M. "The Diversity Scorecard: A Learning Approach to Institutional Change." *Change,* 2004, *36*(1), 45–52.

Bensimon, E. M. "The Underestimated Significance of Practitioner Knowledge in the Scholarship on Student Success." *Review of Higher Education,* 2007, *30*(4), 441–469.

Bensimon, E. M., Hao, L., and Bustillos, L. "Measuring the State of Equity in Higher Education." In P. Gándara, G. Orfield, and C. L. Horn (eds.), *Expanding Opportunity in Higher Education: Leveraging Promise.* Albany: State University of New York Press, 2006.

Bensimon, E. M., Polkinghorne, D. P., Bauman, G. L., and Vallejo, E. "Doing Research That Makes a Difference." *Journal of Higher Education,* 2004, *75*(1), 104–126.

Birnbaum, R. *How Colleges Work: The Cybernetics of Academic Organization and Leadership.* San Francisco: Jossey-Bass, 1988.

Contreras, F. E., Malcom, L. E., and Bensimon, E. M. "An Equity-Based Accountability Framework for Hispanic Serving Institutions." In M. Gasman, B. Baez, and C. Turner (eds.), *Interdisciplinary Approaches to Understanding Minority Serving Institutions.* Albany: State University of New York Press, forthcoming.

Dowd, A. C. *Data Don't Drive: Building a Practitioner-Driven Culture of Inquiry to Assess Community College Performance.* Indianapolis, Ind.: Lumina Foundation for Education, 2005.

Gándara, P. *Priming the Pump: Strategies for Increasing the Achievement of Underrepresented Minority Undergraduates.* Princeton, N.J.: College Board, 1999.

Harper, S. R., and Bensimon, E. M. "Color-Consciousness: A Vital Leadership Quality for Urban College and University Presidents." *UrbanEd,* 2003, *1*(2), 30–32.

Kaplan, R., and Norton, D. "The Balanced Scorecard—Measures That Drive Performance." *Harvard Business Review,* 1992, *70*(1), 71–79.

Massey, D. S., Charles, C. Z., Lundy, G. F., and Fisher, M. J. *The Source of the River: The Social Origins of First-Year Students at America's Selective Colleges and Universities.* Princeton, N.J.: Princeton University Press, 2003.

O'Neil, H. F., Jr., Bensimon, E. M., Diamond, M. A., and Moore, M. R. "Designing and Implementing an Academic Scorecard." *Change,* 1999, *31*(6), 32–41.

Pena, E. V., Bensimon, E. M., and Colyar, J. C. "Contextual Problem Defining: Learning to Think and Act from the Standpoint of Equity." *Liberal Education,* 2006, *92*(2), 48–55.

Steele, C. M. "A Threat in the Air: How Stereotypes Shape Intellectual Identity and Performance." *American Psychologist,* 1997, *52*(6), 613–629.

Wenger, E. *Communities of Practice: Learning, Meaning and Identity.* Cambridge: Cambridge University Press, 1998.

FRANK HARRIS III *is assistant professor of postsecondary education and student affairs at San Diego State University.*

ESTELA MARA BENSIMON *is professor of higher education and director of the Center for Urban Education at the University of Southern California's Rossier School of Education.*

NEW DIRECTIONS FOR STUDENT SERVICES • DOI: 10.1002/ss

7

A historical perspective is offered to explain how race has declined in significance as higher education and student affairs have moved toward multicultural social justice. Educators and administrators are urged to reconsider race and racism in dialogues, programs, policies, and institutional change efforts.

Resituating Race into the Movement Toward Multiculturalism and Social Justice

B. Afeni Cobham, Tara L. Parker

A revisionist history "reexamines America's historical record, replacing comforting majoritarian interpretations of events with ones that square more accurately with minorities' experiences" (Delgado and Stefancic, 2001, p. 21). It demonstrates how racism and racial discrimination were and continue to be staples of American education in large part due to local, state, and federal policies undergirded by racist practices. Such practices are well illustrated in the experiences of marginalized communities of color. For example, in *Deculturalization and the Struggle for Equality* (2001), Spring explained that in the 1800s, legislation in Texas and California declared English the language of instruction in segregated public schools, severely limiting educational opportunities for Latina/o children who were not fluent in English. He also noted that Native American children, removed from their families and tribal traditions, were placed in segregated boarding schools. They were subjected to a curriculum that prescribed English as the standard language, an environment that declared their cultural values uncivilized and inferior to those of the White majority, and teachings that diminished their societal roles to manual laborers. These examples of deeply entrenched subjugation were consistent in the educational experiences of people of color in the United States.

NEW DIRECTIONS FOR STUDENT SERVICES, no. 120, Winter 2007 © Wiley Periodicals, Inc.
Published online in Wiley InterScience (www.interscience.wiley.com) • DOI: 10.1002/ss.260

For communities of color, American education was used as a medium to reinforce oppression through segregation and isolation, forced language requirements, a curriculum rooted in Eurocentric ideals taught by White teachers, and the powerlessness of students of color to express their unique cultural values. The impact of the civil rights movement obligated the federal government to address educational inequities through strategic support programs and services that were conscientious of racial disparities, yet such efforts have never been free from criticism. Today a proverbial spin campaign waged by opponents of race-conscious initiatives characterizes such efforts as reverse discrimination. Colleges and universities, eager to respond to this criticism, "celebrate" diversity in all its forms by highlighting similarities among students as opposed to amplifying their differences. Hosting cultural dinners and ethnic dances and hiring multicultural affairs professionals symbolize a supposed commitment to diversity. Many of these efforts, however, fail to address the deeply layered issue of institutional racism and often dilute race-focused initiatives that are regularly touted under the guise of multiculturalism.

In this chapter, we provide a historical perspective on race in American higher education. We also examine the ways in which racial issues have been supported and confronted on college campuses, as well as how the consideration of race has lost momentum in the light of a movement toward multiculturalism and social justice. In doing so, we offer a cautionary note about negating the historical educational experiences of underrepresented students of color. Such an approach, coupled with legal power struggles over the interpretation of civil rights legislation, has left many in higher education bamboozled. As a result, over the past few years, support services, scholarships, admission policies, and programs designed to level the playing field for historically underrepresented students of color have either been altered to reflect broader notions of diversity or eliminated altogether. Opponents of race-conscious initiatives advance the belief that we live in a colorblind society where academic merit should exclusively be the driving force that determines access to education and other social equity resources.

In this chapter, we challenge these assumptions and call on leaders in student affairs and academic affairs to promote social justice by addressing persistent and prevalent racial issues on college and university campuses. We conclude with recommendations to assist in understanding the current and historical significance and the multiple layers of race in higher education and offer an illustration of how multiculturalism can be realized in a way that resituates race.

A Historical Perspective

For more than forty years, the United States has maintained social policy at the federal and state levels as well as judicial orders to address racial inequality. In higher education, a myriad of diversity awareness and sensitivity trainings have been hosted on campuses across the nation. The issue

NEW DIRECTIONS FOR STUDENT SERVICES • DOI: 10.1002/ss

of race and racism, however, continues to plague our society in general and American higher education in particular. As such, the emphasis, or lack thereof, on race has significant implications for individuals as well as organizations in higher education.

The historic case of *Plessy v. Ferguson* (1896), for example, continues to leave the United States grappling with race and our approach to resolving racial issues in this nation. In 1896, the Supreme Court held that racial segregation on railroads was constitutional provided facilities were "equal." This decision, although specific to railroads, legalized segregation in virtually every service or institution of American life, including restaurants, housing, and education. It was Supreme Court Justice John Marshall Harlan's famous dissenting opinion, however, that is most germane to the evolution of race in the current political climate. Harlan argued, "Our Constitution is colorblind and neither knows nor tolerates classes among citizens. In respect of civil rights, all citizens are equal before the law. . . . The law regards man as man and takes no account of his surroundings or of his color when his civil rights as guaranteed by the supreme law of the land are involved."

While opposing the concept of separate but equal, Harlan's dissent supported the notion of a color-blind society. As a result, those on both sides of racial policy debates have quoted his opinion to buttress their arguments. Many colleges have implemented admissions and retention policies with the underlying principle that a color-blind society actually exists. Indeed, many higher education professionals advocate celebrating student similarities, rather than differences, in efforts to "build community." Community-building initiatives, however, inferred that diversity promulgated a "loss of community" (Martínez Alemán, 2001), as opposed to enhancing it. Furthermore, sensitivity training or diversity awareness programs often resulted in creating politically correct campuses rather than igniting political activism.

The celebrated landmark decision of *Brown v. Board of Education* (1954) legally outlawed racial segregation, yet many predominantly White institutions (PWIs) across the nation failed to admit students of color. As a result, it was not until the 1960s civil rights movement that the doors of PWIs began to open slowly for students of color (Anderson, 2002). In some cases, the doors had to be pried and propped open or even taken off the hinges. In 1961, for example, Charlene Hunter-Gault and Hamilton Holmes arrived at the University of Georgia with the purpose of integrating the institution. Their presence on campus incited racist riots, which prompted the university to suspend both students "for their own safety." Similarly in 1962, federal marshals escorted James Meredith, the first Black student to enroll at the University of Mississippi, to campus. A riot ensued, the campus was set afire, and two students were killed (Anderson, 2002).

Often state officials chose to close public colleges rather than to desegregate, let alone integrate, them. Many, laws that attempted to desegregate education, create access, and promote equity failed to eradicate the spirit of inherent racism that persisted in college student life, student interactions, institutional policy, employment, and pedagogy. It became apparent that PWIs were not created to facilitate a holistic educational experience for non-White Americans or immigrant people of color. Many students of color attending PWIs found the campuses to be alienating or unwelcoming. Confronted with real or perceived racial discrimination, overt racism, and few mentors on campus, they formed groups under the banner of student activism in an effort to cope with these conditions and address issues internal and external to university communities (Patton, 2006). The foundation of ethnic mobilization on college campuses derived from two sources: the political tone of America in the 1960s, and the Black power movement. Ogbar (2005) explains, "Black Power [did not] advocate for white acceptance. . . . It affirmed Black people, their history, their beauty and set them at the center of their worldview. It approved Black anger at the vicious cycle of white supremacy . . . [and] declared Black people's right to autonomous space within white-controlled domains" (p. 156).

With little administrative support, Black students, as well as other racial/ethnic student groups, took matters into their own hands and demanded a change in the campus climate and the resources afforded to students. Consequently, organizations like black student unions emerged to help make PWIs more hospitable and reflective of the cultural wealth Black students brought to campus. Several communities of color borrowed from the political agency of Black student unions and began to form similar organizations. Between 1968 and 1969 several Chicano student organizations emerged to advance a Chicano civil rights movement that illuminated the atrocities Mexican Americans suffered in areas of education, employment, and land ownership. The Asian American Political Alliance, founded at the University of California, Berkeley, called for an end to the Vietnam War and the exploitation of Asian farmworkers and sought to eradicate the stereotype of the model minority. The National Indian Youth Council and the Native American Student Association led the red power movement. According to Ogbar (2005) these groups used college campuses to bring awareness to the plight of Native Americans as "rates of alcoholism, high school dropout, unemployment and death were higher for them than for any other group in the country" (p. 176).

In addition to their own student-run organizations, students of color petitioned and protested for increases in faculty of color, ethnic studies departments, and separate campus facilities (Patton, 2006; Williamson, 1999). New faculty brought new ideas and new scholarship. Many helped to establish Black studies departments as part of a larger political objective. Through Black and other ethnic studies programs, faculty served as "instruments with which oppressed peoples could learn to change society" (Williamson, 1999, p. 98). The significance of emerging Black studies programs thus extended beyond a simple change in the academic offerings of an institution. Students from all racial/ethnic backgrounds protested and fought for these programs in the name of democracy and social justice. As a result, Black studies programs were successful examples of multiracial

NEW DIRECTIONS FOR STUDENT SERVICES • DOI: 10.1002/ss

activism toward social justice. Brooks (2006), however, argued that despite nearly five hundred Black studies departments and programs on today's college campuses, they are rarely linked to the collective struggle of eradicating persistent social inequalities and racial disparities. The perceived purpose of these programs therefore seems to have changed. Perceptions of these programs as glorified affirmative action initiatives have left Black studies departments and their faculties in a constant struggle to prove intellectual legitimacy (Villalpando and Bernal, 2002) and circumvent mergers into larger academic programs as an interdisciplinary minor.

Moreover, Omi and Winant (1994) argued that educational programs and practices of the 1960s were gradually dissolved, dispersed, and defused. Initiatives associated with affirmative action, for example, began spiraling downward in 1978 when Allan Bakke sued the University of California Medical School for reserving sixteen spaces out of one hundred for historically underrepresented students of color (Bowen and Bok, 1998). The outcome of the case became a legal tipping point in the crusade to dismantle similar programs at colleges and universities. As this was true in the access arena, we see numerous other examples of how campuses have followed suit.

Loss of Momentum in the Movement

These historic racial realities beckon leaders in higher education to acknowledge, confront, and appropriately respond to the idea that the social construction of race has created systemic provisions that exclude all non-Whites from full citizenship, ultimately creating two worlds within one society—those who are privileged and those who are not—exclusively based on race (Spring, 2001). Moreover, Omi and Winant (1994) suggested that by reducing race to a single component of a larger diversity umbrella, higher education policymakers and institutional leaders may fail to recognize the sociohistorical, political, and economic significance of race. Indeed, there are several circumstances that can be attributed at least in part to the declining significance of race in the movement toward multiculturalism. In the following sections, we briefly discuss five examples that demonstrate the momentum lost in the ongoing fight for racial justice in higher education.

From Affirmative Action to Negative Reaction. Forty-two years after the passage of the 1965 Civil Rights Act, an anonymous Web blogger asked, "How long must we pay for the sins of racism?" In our view, this question suggests the following: feeling cheated by affirmative action and equal opportunity programs, believing these programs have already repaid the debt of past racism and discrimination, and no longer perceiving race as problematic due to a visible increase in structural diversity. In contrast, we argue that the admission of underrepresented students of color is not indicative of a thriving multicultural community. Instead, higher education has become the battleground for calculated assaults on initiatives that were designed to expand access and provide some degree of social justice.

In 1997, Barbara Grutter sued the University of Michigan Law School for considering race in its admissions decisions. Like Bakke, the plaintiff and those who supported her case failed to acknowledge that the past transgressions of racism were in direct correlation with cyclical and long-standing access issues that kept racial/ethnic minorities underrepresented (Solórzano and Yosso, 2002). A recent report published by the American Council on Education found that over the past thirteen years, White women outpaced White men and men and women from all other racial/ethnic groups in the category of conferred bachelor degrees (King, 2006). Notwithstanding, after the *Grutter* decision, several institutions altered the original objectives of equal opportunity programs through broadened diversity programs that included a wide range of populations, while others eradicated these initiatives altogether, citing fear of legal reprisal under the guise of reverse discrimination.

Schmidt (2006) provided several examples of the deracialization of programs and initiatives on campuses across the country. At Cornell University several offices in the undergraduate schools removed the word *minority* from their programs or services and began to use broad labels like *diversity* or *multicultural*. Tufts University altered the eligibility of a summer research program by making it available to economically disadvantaged students as opposed to maintaining its focus on underrepresented students of color. Washington University changed criteria for a scholarship program originally aimed at students of color by making it available to "students who demonstrate leadership potential." In addition, the Andrew Mellon Foundation and National Institutes of Health ceased financial support to college programs that factored race in the selection criteria (Schmidt, 2006). Most recently, an independent research organization in support of fiscal accountability demanded a strict accounting of funds spent on diversity initiatives at the University of Colorado-Boulder. It is compelling that this same group has not sought accountability of expenditures related to athletic recruitment, courtship of alumni children, or the family members of high-end benefactors.

Reverse Discrimination or Cultural Capital? *Cultural capital* is defined as "the knowledge, skills, education, and advantages a person has that make the educational system a comfortable, familiar environment in which he or she can succeed easily" (Oldfield, 2007, p. 2). In the larger scheme, most underrepresented students of color enrolled at PWIs have less access than their White counterparts to resources and relationships with peers, faculty, and staff who possess cultural capital. As a result, students of color participate in ethnic organizations, Black fraternities and sororities, and other groups or offices, otherwise known as counterspaces (Solórzano, Ceja, and Yosso, 2000), that purposefully take race into consideration. Counterspaces allow students to engage their racial identities, focusing attention on self-discovery and discarding internalized stereotypes about one's own group.

Critics, however, have argued that institutional support for ethnic organizations, departments, and racially divided facilities was counterproductive to cross-racial engagement and "legitimized a regime of double

NEW DIRECTIONS FOR STUDENT SERVICES • DOI: 10.1002/ss

standards that divides and Balkanizes the campus" (D'Souza, 1992, p. 242). In 2002, a group that espouses to be "the voice of sanity about race and civil rights" argued that an institution's commitment to increase ethnic communities is "contradicted by on-campus segregation that is college-sponsored" (Meyers, Mohajer, and Sung, 2002, p. 4). This criticism illustrates the contradictory social practices and perceptions that continue to polarize racial inequality at PWIs. Criticism of racial/ethnic communities that choose to come together for support, social networking, the exploration of their own cultural identities, and the cultivation of cultural capital is both compelling and all too familiar. In stark contrast, White students are not subjected to such criticism when they choose to remain in familiar comfort zones that cluster them in predominantly White fraternities and sororities, athletic teams, student government, religious cultural centers, theme housing centered on European culture, and in every other facet of the university social setting. Furthermore, research shows that White students are less open to interracial engagement and withdraw from opportunities to interact with students of other racial/ethnic backgrounds (Balenger, Hoffman, and Sedlacek, 1992; Steward, Davidson, and Borgers, 1993).

Reinserting Race into Movement at Institutions

As Lori Patton, Marylu McEwen, Laura Rendón, and Mary Howard-Hamilton noted in Chapter Three, critical race theory (CRT) has the potential of illuminating racially inept institutional practices. CRT offers epistemological space to study and learn from the cultural capital that students of color bring with them from their socialized experiences. CRT as a framework creates an opportunity for educators and administrators to foster campus climates that facilitate learning from an array of "cultural knowledge, skills, abilities and contacts possessed by socially marginalized groups" (Yosso, 2005, p. 69). Yosso also asserts that CRT is beneficial in educational settings because it shifts the view of socially marginalized communities as hopelessly disadvantaged and culturally deficient. Furthermore, CRT offers a lens through which to develop and advocate for institutional practices that simultaneously situate race and multiculturalism in every facet of the campus culture.

This can be accomplished, in some measure, by acknowledging that race and issues of racism are embedded in American history (Spring, 2001). As such, postsecondary institutions must develop "cultures of inquiry" (Dowd, 2005) that promote the continual assessment of policies, practices, norms, and data disaggregated by race. Scholars have argued that educators and decision makers in higher education must be aware of the differences among underrepresented groups and not compress them into a meaningless whole (Graves, 1990; Wilkerson, 1987; Yosso, 2005). In other words, it is the responsibility of institutional leaders and policymakers to acknowledge that while some issues may be universal to underrepresented students, there are many issues that are not and therefore require heightened attention.

NEW DIRECTIONS FOR STUDENT SERVICES • DOI: 10.1002/ss

Responding to the realities of race requires skillfully and consciously multi-tasking the multiple dimensions of multiculturalism without compromising one for the other. Social justice on behalf of all marginalized and oppressed groups requires serious institutional effort. Notwithstanding, reinserting race into dialogues, actions, critiques, and scholarship is essential, especially given that race has been socially constructed for each student who attends and every person who works on a college or university campus.

References

Anderson, J. D. "Race in American Higher Education: Historical Perspectives on Current Conditions." In W. Smith, P. G. Altbach, and K. Lomotey (eds.), *The Racial Crisis in American Higher Education: Continuing Challenges for the Twenty-First Century.* (2nd ed.) Albany: State University of New York Press, 2002.

Bakke v. Regents of the University of California, 553 P.2d 1152 (Cal. 1976).

Balenger, V. J., Hoffman, M. A., and Sedlacek, W. E. "Racial Attitudes Among Incoming White Students: A Study of Ten-Year Trends." *Journal of College Student Development,* 1992, *33,* 245–252.

Bowen, W. G., and Bok, D. *The Shape of the River: Long-Term Consequences of Considering Race in College and University Admissions.* Princeton, N.J.: Princeton University Press, 1998.

Brooks, N. M. "The Beginnings of Black Studies." *Chronicle of Higher Education,* Feb. 10, 2006, p. B8.

Brown v. Board of Education, 347 U.S. 483. 1954.

Delgado, R., and Stefancic, J. *Critical Race Theory: An Introduction.* New York: New York University Press, 2001.

Dowd, A. *Data Don't Drive: Building a Practitioner-Driven Culture of Inquiry to Assess Community College Performance.* Indianapolis, Ind.: Lumina Foundation for Education, 2005.

D'Souza, D. *Illiberal Education: The Politics of Race and Sex on Campus.* New York: Vintage Books, 1992.

Graves, S. B. "A Case of Double Jeopardy? Black Women in Higher Education." *Initiatives,* 1990, *53*(1), 3–8.

Grutter v. Bollinger, 124 35 (S. Ct. 2003).

King, J. *Gender Equity in Higher Education: 2006.* Washington, D.C.: American Council on Education, 2006.

Martínez Alemán, A. M. "Community, Higher Education, and the Challenge of Multiculturalism." *Teachers College Record,* 2001, *103,* 485–503.

Meyers, M., Mohajer, R. A., and Sung, E. *The Stigma of Inclusion: Racial Paternalism/ Separatism in Higher Education.* New York: New York Civil Rights Coalition, 2002.

Ogbar, J. *Black Power: Radical Politics and Black Identity.* Baltimore, Md.: Johns Hopkins University Press, 2005.

Oldfield, K. "Humble and Hopeful: Welcoming First Generation Poor and Working Class Students to College." *About Campus,* 2007, *11*(6) 2–12.

Omi, M., and Winant, H. *Racial Formation in the United States: From the 1960s to the 1990s.* (2nd ed.) New York: Routledge, 1994.

Patton, L. D. "The Voice of Reason: A Qualitative Examination of Black Student Perceptions of Black Culture Centers." *Journal of College Student Development,* 2006, *47*(6), 628–644.

Plessy v. Ferguson. 163 U.S. 537. 1896.

Schmidt, P. "From 'Minority' to 'Diversity': The Transformation of Formerly Race-Exclusive Programs May Be Leaving Some Students Out in the Cold." *Chronicle of Higher Education,* Feb. 3, 2006, p. A24.

Solórzano, D. G., Ceja, M., and Yosso, T. "Critical Race Theory, Racial Microaggressions, and Campus Racial Climate: The Experiences of African American College Students." *Journal of Negro Education,* 2000, *69*(1), 60–73.

Solórzano, D. G., and Yosso, T. J. "A Critical Race Counterstory of Race, Racism and Affirmative Action." *Equity and Excellence in Education,* 2002, *35*(2), 155–168.

Spring, J. *Deculturalization and the Struggle for Equality: A Brief History of the Education of Dominated Cultures in the United States.* (3rd ed.) New York: McGraw-Hill, 2001.

Steward, R. J., Davidson, J. A., and Borgers, S. A. "Racial Majority vs. Minority Status: A Study of Interactional Styles of Successful White Students on a Predominantly White University Campus." *Journal of College Student Development,* 1993, *34*, 295–299.

Villalpando, O., and Bernal, D. D. "A Critical Race Theory Analysis of Barriers That Impede the Success of Faculty of Color." In W. A. Smith, P. G. Altbach, and K. Lomotey (eds.), *The Racial Crisis in American Higher Education.* (2nd ed.) Albany: State University of New York Press, 2002.

Wilkerson, M. B. "How Equal Is Equal Education: Race, Class and Gender." In C. Lasser (ed.), *Educating Men and Women Together: Coeducation in a Changing World.* Chicago: University of Illinois Press, 1987.

Williamson, J. A. "In Defense of Themselves: The Black Student Struggle for Success and Recognition at Predominantly White Colleges and Universities." *Journal of Negro Education,* 1999, *68*(1), 92–105.

Yosso, T. J. "Whose Culture Has Capital? A Critical Race Theory Discussion of Community Cultural Wealth." *Race, Ethnicity and Education,* 2005, *8*(1), 69–91.

B. AFENI COBHAM is assistant provost for student life at the University of Denver.

TARA L. PARKER is assistant professor of higher education at the University of Massachusetts, Boston.

INDEX

Abes, E. S., 39, 40, 41
Academic Scorecard for Higher Education, 79
Affirmative action programs, 89–90
Allen, W. R., 12, 20, 29, 30, 69, 70, 71
Allport, G., 28
American Council on Education, 90
Ancis, J. R., 12
Anderson, J. D., 87
Andrew Mellon Foundation, 90
Antonio, A. L., 14, 16, 27, 28
Apple, M. W., 41
Applying New Developmental Findings (Knefelkamp, Widick, and Parker), 40
Artificial integration: addressing issue of, 34–36; definition of, 34
Asian American Political Alliance, 88
Asian American students: lack of research on racial climate and, 12; multicampus qualitative study of racial climates and, 15–19. *See also* Minority students
Association of American Colleges and Universities, 27
Astin, A. W., 14, 28, 33
Atkinson, D. R., 41

Bakke, A., 89, 90
Bakke v. Regents of the University of California, 27
Balanced Scorecard, 79
Baldwin, J., 41
Balenger, V. J., 91
Bauman, G. L., 78, 80, 81, 83
Baxter Magolda, M. B., 4, 40, 42, 55, 58, 66
Belenky, M. F., 63, 64
Bell, D., 3
Bensimon, E. M., 4, 31, 77, 78, 79, 80, 81, 83, 84
Berger, J. B., 28
Bergerson, A. A., 3
Birnbaum, R., 78
Bishop, A., 72
Black identity development models, 40
Black Power, 88
Black students: affirmative action programs and, 89–90; multicampus qualitative study of racial climates and,

15–19; self-reports of racial segregation by, 16–17. *See also* Minority students
Bok, D., 89
Bollinger, Gratz v. , 14, 26
Bollinger, Grutter v. , 14, 26, 27, 90
Bond, L. A., 64
Borgers, S. A., 91
Bourdieu, P., 33
Bowen, W. g., 89
Brooks, N. M., 89
Brown, O. G., 42
Brown v. Board of Education, 87
Bryant, D. R., 43
Bustillos, L., 77, 81

Cabrera, A. F., 12
"The Campus Racial Climate: Contexts of Conflict" (Hurtado), 9
Campus racial climates: benefits associated with cross-racial engagement, 14; color-blind environment and, 68–70; differential perceptions by race, 12; experiences across the country with, 7–9; implications for institutional transformation of, 19–21; minority student reports on, 12–14; multicampus qualitative study of, 15–19; post-1992 research on, 9–15. *See also* Higher education
Carter, D. F., 13
Ceja, M., 12, 14, 15, 45, 90
Center for Urban Education (USC), 78
Chang, J., 26, 35
Chang, M. J., 4, 14, 25, 26, 29, 33, 34, 35, 37
Charles, C. Z., 78
Chicano civil rights movement, 88
Chickering, A. W., 40, 41, 43
CIRP (Cooperative Institutional Research Program), 9
Civil Rights Act (1965), 89
Clayton-Pedersen, A., 20, 29, 30, 69, 70, 71
Clinchy, B. M., 63
Cobham, B. A., 4, 85, 93
Color-blind racism, 68–70
Colyar, J. C., 78, 80, 81
Contreras, F. E., 79

SS116 The Small College Dean
Sarah B. Westfall
Senior student affairs professionals in small colleges have their own
challenges and rewards that are often overlooked by the literature. This
volume's authors give insight to working at colleges with fewer than 5,000
students, with chapters about the dean's portfolio, recruiting and retaining
staff, academic vs. student affairs, the vice president's role, and more. This
volume is a primer on serving as a dean at a small college.
ISBN: 0-7879-9580-0

SS115 Supporting Graduate and Professional Students
Melanie J. Guentzel, Becki Elkins Nesheim
Student affairs practice has historically focused on undergraduates and left
support (academic, social, professional) for graduate students to their
respective department or college. But academic departments emphasize
cognitive development of a scholar rather than the psychosocial aspects of
the graduate student experience. This volume focuses on the needs of
graduate and professional students that can be addressed specifically by
student affairs professionals.
ISBN: 0-7879-9057-4

SS114 Understanding Students in Transition: Trends and Issues
Frankie Santos Laanan
This volume is designed for practitioners (in student services, teaching, or
administration) seeking to understand the changing realities of today's
diverse, complex college students. It includes recommendations for research,
practice, and policy. The research and practical examples can be applied to
multiple student populations: recent high school graduates, community
college transfers, and older adults returning to education.
ISBN: 0-7879-8679-8

SS113 Gambling on Campus
George S. McClellan, Thomas W. Hardy, Jim Caswell
Gambling has become a serious concern on college campuses, fueled by the
surge of online gaming and the national poker craze, and is no longer a
fringe activity. This informative issue includes perspectives from students,
suggestions for research, frameworks for campus policy development, and
case studies of education and intervention. Anyone interested in supporting
student success must be informed about gambling on campus.
ISBN: 0-7879-8597-X

SS112 Technology in Student Affairs: Supporting Student Learning and Services
Kevin Kruger
Information technology has helped create a 24/7 self-service way for
students to interact with campus administrative functions, whether they're
on campus or distance learners. And new technologies could move beyond
administrative into student learning and development. This volume is not a
review of current technology in student affairs. Rather, it focuses on how
technology is changing the organization of student affairs, how to use it
effectively, and how lines are blurring between campus-based and distance
learning.
ISBN: 0-7879-8362-4

**SS111 Gender Identity and Sexual Orientation: Research, Policy, and Personal
Perspectives**
Ronni L. Sanlo
Lesbian, gay, bisexual, and transgender people have experienced
homophobia, discrimination, exclusion, and marginalization in the academy,
from subtle to overt. Yet LGBT people have been a vital part of the history of

American higher education. This volume describes current issues, research, and policies, and it offers ways for institutions to support and foster the success of LGBT students, faculty, and staff.
ISBN: 0-7879-8328-4

SS110   **Developing Social Justice Allies**
Robert D. Reason, Ellen M. Broido, Tracy L. Davis, Nancy J. Evans
Social justice allies are individuals from dominant groups (for example, whites, heterosexuals, men) who work to end the oppression of target group members (people of color, homosexuals, women). Student affairs professionals have a history of philosophical commitment to social justice, and this volume strives to provide the theoretical foundation and practical strategies to encourage the development of social justice and civil rights allies among students and colleagues.
ISBN: 0-7879-8077-3

SS109   **Serving Native American Students**
Mary Jo Tippeconnic Fox, Shelly C. Lowe, George S. McClellan
The increasing Native American enrollment on campuses nationwide is something to celebrate; however, the retention rate for Native American students is the lowest in higher education, a point of tremendous concern. This volume's authors—most of them Native American—address topics such as enrollment trends, campus experiences, cultural traditions, student services, ignorance about Indian country issues, expectations of tribal leaders and parents, and other challenges and opportunities encountered by Native students.
ISBN: 0-7879-7971-6

SS108   **Using Entertainment Media in Student Affairs Teaching and Practice**
Deanna S. Forney, Tony W. Cawthon
Reaching all students may require going beyond traditional methods, especially in the out-of-classroom environments typical to student affairs. Using films, music, television shows, and popular books can help students learn. This volume—good for both practitioners and educators—shares effective approaches to using entertainment media to facilitate understanding of general student development, multiculturalism, sexual orientation, gender issues, leadership, counseling, and more.
ISBN: 0-7879-7926-0

SS107   **Developing Effective Programs and Services for College Men**
Gar E. Kellom
This volume's aim is to better understand the challenges facing college men, particularly at-risk men. Topics include enrollment, retention, academic performance, women's college perspectives, men's studies perspectives, men's health issues, emotional development, and spirituality. Chapters deliver recommendations and examples about programs and services that improve college men's learning experiences and race, class, and gender awareness.
ISBN: 0-7879-7772-1

SS106   **Serving the Millennial Generation**
Michael D. Coomes, Robert DeBard
Focuses on the next enrollment boom, students born after 1981, known as the Millennial generation. Examines these students' attitudes, beliefs, and behaviors, and makes recommendations to student affairs practitioners for working with them. Discusses historical and cultural influences that shape generations, demographics, teaching and learning patterns of Millennials, and how student affairs can best educate and serve them.
ISBN: 0-7879-7606-7

SS105   Addressing the Unique Needs of Latino American Students
Anna M. Ortiz
Explores the experiences of the fast-growing population of Latinos in higher
education, and what these students need from student affairs. This volume
examines the influence of the Latino family, socioeconomic levels, cultural
barriers, and other factors to understand the challenges faced by Latinos.
Discusses administration, student groups, community colleges, support
programs, cultural identity, Hispanic-Serving Institutions, and more.
ISBN: 0-7879-7479-X

SS104   Meeting the Needs of African American Women
Mary F. Howard-Hamilton
Identifies and explores the critical needs for African American women as
students, faculty, and administrators. This volume introduces theoretical
frameworks and practical applications for addressing challenges; discusses
identity and spirituality; explores the importance of programming support in
recruitment and retention; describes the benefits of mentoring; and provides
illuminating case studies of black women's issues in higher education.
ISBN: 0-7879-7280-0

SS103   Contemporary Financial Issues in Student Affairs
John H. Schuh
This volume addresses the challenging financial situation facing higher
education and offers creative solutions for student affairs staff. Topics
include the differences between public and private institutions in funding
student activities, how to demonstrate financial accountability to
stakeholders, plus ways to address budget challenges in student unions,
health centers, campus recreation, counseling centers, and student housing.
ISBN: 0-7879-7173-1

SS102   Meeting the Special Needs of Adult Students
Deborah Kilgore, Penny J. Rice
This volume examines the ways student services professionals can best help
adult learners. Chapters highlight the specific challenges that adult enrollment brings to traditional four-year and postgraduate institutions, which are
often focused on the traditional-aged student experience. Explaining that
adult students are typically involved in campus life in different ways than
younger students are, the volume provides student services professionals with
good guidance on serving an ever-growing population.
ISBN: 0-7879-6991-5

SS101   Planning and Achieving Successful Student Affairs Facilities Projects
Jerry Price
Provides student affairs professionals with an examination of critical
facilities issues by exploring the experiences of their colleagues. Illustrates
that students' educational experiences are affected by residence halls,
student unions, dining services, recreation and wellness centers, and campus
grounds, and that student affairs professionals make valuable contributions
to the success of campus facility projects. Covers planning, budgeting,
collaboration, and communication through case studies and lessons learned.
ISBN: 0-7879-6847-1

SS100   Student Affairs and External Relations
Mary Beth Snyder
Building positive relations with external constituents is as important in
student affairs work as it is in any other university or college division. This
issue is a long-overdue resource of ideas, strategies, and information aimed
at making student affairs leaders more effective in their interactions with

important off-campus partners, supporters, and agencies. Chapter authors explore the current challenges facing the student services profession as well as the emerging opportunities worthy of student affairs interest.
ISBN: 0-7879-6342-9

SS99   **Addressing Contemporary Campus Safety Issues**
Christine K. Wilkinson, James A. Rund
Provided for practitioners as a resource book for both historical and evolving issues, this guide covers hazing, parental partnerships, and collaborative relationships between universities and the neighboring community. Addressing a new definition of a safe campus environment, the editors have identified topics such as the growth in study abroad, the implications of increased usage of technology on campus, and campus response to September 11. In addition, large-scale crisis responses to student riots and multiple campus tragedies have been described in case studies. The issue speaks to a more contemporary definition of a safe campus environment that addresses not only physical safety issues but also those of a psychological nature, a more diverse student body, and quality of life.
ISBN: 0-7879-6341-0

SS98   **The Art and Practical Wisdom of Student Affairs Leadership**
Jon Dalton, Marguerite McClinton
This issue collects reflections, stories, and advice about the art and practice of student affairs leadership. Ten senior student affairs leaders were asked to maintain a journal and record their personal reflections on practical wisdom they have gained in the profession. The authors looked inside themselves to provide personal and candid insight into the convictions and values that have guided them in their work and lives.
ISBN: 0-7879-6340-2

SS97   **Working with Asian American College Students**
Marylu K. McEwen, Corinne Maekawa Kodama, Alvin N. Alvarez, Sunny Lee, Christopher T. H. Liang
Highlights the diversity of Asian American college students, analyzes the "model minority" myth and the stereotype of the "perfidious foreigner," and points out the need to consider the racial identity and racial consciousness of Asian American students. Various authors propose a model of Asian American student development, address issues of Asian Americans who are at educational risk, discuss the importance of integration and collaboration between student affairs and Asian American studies programs, and offer strategies for developing socially conscious Asian American student leaders.
ISBN: 0-7879-6292-9S

NEW DIRECTIONS FOR STUDENT SERVICES
Order Form
SUBSCRIPTIONS AND SINGLE ISSUES

DISCOUNTED BACK ISSUES:

Use this form to receive **20% off** all back issues of New Directions for Student Services. All single issues priced at **$22.40** (normally $28.00)

TITLE	ISSUE NO.	ISBN
_____	_____	_____
_____	_____	_____
_____	_____	_____

Call 888-378-2537 or see mailing instructions below. When calling, mention the promotional code, JB7ND, to receive your discount.

SUBSCRIPTIONS: *(1 year, 4 issues)*

☐ New Order   ☐ Renewal

U.S.	☐ Individual: $80	☐ Institutional: $195
Canada/Mexico	☐ Individual: $80	☐ Institutional: $235
All Others	☐ Individual: $104	☐ Institutional: $269

Call 888-378-2537 or see mailing and pricing instructions below. Online subscriptions are available at www.interscience.wiley.com.

Copy or detach page and send to:
John Wiley & Sons, Journals Dept, 5th Floor
989 Market Street, San Francisco, CA 94103-1741
Order Form can also be faxed to: 888-481-2665

Issue/Subscription Amount: $ _____	**SHIPPING CHARGES:**		
Shipping Amount: $ _____	SURFACE	Domestic	Canadian
(for single issues only—subscription prices include shipping)	First Item	$5.00	$6.00
Total Amount: $ _____	Each Add'l Item	$3.00	$1.50

(No sales tax for U.S. subscriptions. Canadian residents, add GST for subscription orders. Individual rate subscriptions must be paid by personal check or credit card. Individual rate subscriptions may not be resold as library copies.)

☐ Payment enclosed (U.S. check or money order only. All payments must be in U.S. dollars.)

☐ VISA ☐ MC ☐ Amex # _____ Exp. Date _____

Card Holder Name _____ Card Issue # _____

Signature _____ Day Phone _____

☐ Bill Me (U.S. institutional orders only. Purchase order required.)

Purchase order # _____

Federal Tax ID13559302   GST 89102 8052

Name _____

Address _____

Phone _____ E-mail _____

JB7ND

**NEW DIRECTIONS FOR STUDENT SERVICES
IS NOW AVAILABLE ONLINE AT WILEY INTERSCIENCE**

What is Wiley InterScience?

Wiley InterScience is the dynamic online content service from John Wiley & Sons delivering the full text of over 300 leading scientific, technical, medical, and professional journals, plus major reference works, the acclaimed *Current Protocols* laboratory manuals, and even the full text of select Wiley print books online.

What are some special features of Wiley InterScience?

Wiley InterScience Alerts is a service that delivers table of contents via e-mail for any journal available on Wiley InterScience as soon as a new issue is published online.
Early View is Wiley's exclusive service presenting individual articles online as soon as they are ready, even before the release of the compiled print issue. These articles are complete, peer-reviewed, and citable.
CrossRef is the innovative multi-publisher reference linking system enabling readers to move seamlessly from a reference in a journal article to the cited publication, typically located on a different server and published by a different publisher.

How can I access Wiley InterScience?

Visit http://www.interscience.wiley.com

Guest Users can browse Wiley InterScience for unrestricted access to journal Tables of Contents and Article Abstracts, or use the powerful search engine.
Registered Users are provided with a *Personal Home Page* to store and manage customized alerts, searches, and links to favorite journals and articles. Additionally, Registered Users can view free Online Sample Issues and preview selected material from major reference works.
Licensed Customers are entitled to access full-text journal articles in PDF, with select journals also offering full-text HTML.

How do I become an Authorized User?

Authorized Users are individuals authorized by a paying Customer to have access to the journals in Wiley InterScience. For example, a university that subscribes to Wiley journals is considered to be the Customer. Faculty, staff and students authorized by the university to have access to those journals in Wiley InterScience are Authorized Users. Users should contact their Library for information on which Wiley journals they have access to in Wiley InterScience.

ASK YOUR INSTITUTION ABOUT WILEY INTERSCIENCE TODAY!

1. Publication Title	2. Publication Number										3. Filing Date
New Directions for Student Services	0	1	6	4	_	7	9	7	0		10/1/2007

4. Issue Frequency	5. Number of Issues Published Annually	6. Annual Subscription Price
Quarterly	4	$209

7. Complete Mailing Address of Known Office of Publication (Not printer) (Street, city, county, state, and ZIP+4®)	Contact Person
Wiley Subscriptions Services, Inc. at Jossey-Bass, 989 Market St., San Francisco, CA 94103	Joe Schuman
	Telephone (Include area code) 415-782-3232

8. Complete Mailing Address of Headquarters or General Business Office of Publisher (Not printer)

Wiley Subscriptions Services, Inc., 111 River Street, Hoboken, NJ 07030

9. Full Names and Complete Mailing Addresses of Publisher, Editor, and Managing Editor (Do not leave blank)
Publisher (Name and complete mailing address)

Wiley Subscriptions Services, Inc., A Wiley Company at San Francisco, 989 Market St., San Francisco, CA 94103-1741

Editor (Name and complete mailing address)

John H. Schuh, N243 Lagomarcino Hall, Iowa State University, Ames, IA 50011

Managing Editor (Name and complete mailing address)

None

10. Owner (Do not leave blank. If the publication is owned by a corporation, give the name and address of the corporation immediately followed by the names and addresses of all stockholders owning or holding 1 percent or more of the total amount of stock. If not owned by a corporation, give the names and addresses of the individual owners. If owned by a partnership or other unincorporated firm, give its name and address as well as those of each individual owner. If the publication is published by a nonprofit organization, give its name and address.)

Full Name	Complete Mailing Address
Wiley Subscriptions Services	111 River Street, Hoboken, NJ
(see attached list)	

11. Known Bondholders, Mortgagees, and Other Security Holders Owning or Holding 1 Percent or More of Total Amount of Bonds, Mortgages, or Other Securities. If none, check box ▶ ☑ None

Full Name	Complete Mailing Address

12. Tax Status (For completion by nonprofit organizations authorized to mail at nonprofit rates) (Check one)
The purpose, function, and nonprofit status of this organization and the exempt status for federal income tax purposes:
☐ Has Not Changed During Preceding 12 Months
☐ Has Changed During Preceding 12 Months (Publisher must submit explanation of change with this statement)

13. Publication Title	14. Issue Date for Circulation Data
New Directions for Student Services	Summer 2007

15. Extent and Nature of Circulation		Average No. Copies Each Issue During Preceding 12 Months	No. Copies of Single Issue Published Nearest to Filing Date
a. Total Number of Copies (Net press run)		1459	1302
b. Paid Circulation (By Mail and Outside the Mail)	(1) Mailed Outside-County Paid Subscriptions Stated on PS Form 3541 (Include paid distribution above nominal rate, advertiser's proof copies, and exchange copies)	431	417
	(2) Mailed In-County Paid Subscriptions Stated on PS Form 3541 (Include paid distribution above nominal rate, advertiser's proof copies, and exchange copies)	0	0
	(3) Paid Distribution Outside the Mails Including Sales Through Dealers and Carriers, Street Vendors, Counter Sales, and Other Paid Distribution Outside USPS®	0	0
	(4) Paid Distribution by Other Classes of Mail Through the USPS (e.g. First-Class Mail®)	0	0
c. Total Paid Distribution (Sum of 15b (1), (2),(3), and (4))		431	417
d. Free or Nominal Rate Distribution (By Mail and Outside the Mail)	(1) Free or Nominal Rate Outside-County Copies Iincluded on PS Form 3541	88	87
	(2) Free or Nominal Rate In-County Copies Included on PS Form 3541	0	0
	(3) Free or Nominal Rate Copies Mailed at Other Classes Through the USPS (e.g. First-Class Mail)	0	0
	(4) Free or Nominal Rate Distribution Outside the Mail (Carriers or other means)	0	0
e. Total Free or Nominal Rate Distribution (Sum of 15d (1), (2), (3) and (4))		88	87
f. Total Distribution (Sum of 15c and 15e) ▶		519	504
g. Copies not Distributed (See Instructions to Publishers #4 (page #3)) ▶		940	798
h. Total (Sum of 15f and g) ▶		1459	1302
i. Percent Paid (15c divided by 15f times 100) ▶		83%	83%

16. Publication of Statement of Ownership

☑ If the publication is a general publication, publication of this statement is required. Will be printed
in the WINTER 2007 issue of this publication.

☐ Publication not required.

17. Signature and Title of Editor, Publisher, Business Manager, or Owner	Date
Susan E. Lewis, VP & Publisher /Periodicals _Susan Lewis_	10/1/2007

I certify that all information furnished on this form is true and complete. I understand that anyone who furnishes false or misleading information on this form or who omits material or information requested on the form may be subject to criminal sanctions (including fines and imprisonment) and/or civil sanctions (including civil penalties).